365 Days of Wisdom

Daily Messages and Practical Contemplations
to Inspire You Throughout the Year

365 Days of Wisdom

Daily Messages and Practical Contemplations
to Inspire You Throughout the Year

Dadi Janki

BOOKS

Winchester, UK
Washington, USA

First published by O-Books, 2011
O-Books is an imprint of John Hunt Publishing Ltd., Laurel House, Station Approach,
Alresford, Hants, SO24 9JH, UK
office1@o-books.net
www.o-books.com

For distributor details and how to order please visit the 'Ordering' section on our website.

Text copyright: Dadi Janki 2011

ISBN: 978 1 84694 863 3

A CIP catalogue record for this book is available from the British Library.

Design: Lee Nash
Cover: Stuart Davies
www.stuartdaviesart.com

Printed in the UK by CPI Antony Rowe
Printed in the USA by Offset Paperback Mfrs, Inc

We operate a distinctive and ethical publishing philosophy in all
areas of our business, from our global network of authors to
production and worldwide distribution.

THANKS TO BRAHMA KUMARIS BUSINESS AND INDUSTRY WING, JVPD SCHEME, MUMBAI, INDIA.

FOREWORD

The world will automatically become a better place when each individual becomes a better person – and this book of thoughts, one for each day of the year, will show you how to become a better person day by day. For each day of the year you will find an inspiring quotation, a contemplation and ways to put those thoughts into practical action in your life.

All these thoughts are based on twelve core values: co-operation, freedom, happiness, honesty, humility, love, peace, respect, responsibility, simplicity, tolerance and unity. These are the values we all need to cultivate to become better individuals, but they are also fundamental to the well-being of humanity as a whole.

We might think of these founding values as providing the fertile ground in which we can plant seeds which are sure to bear fruit. That fruit is the growth of eight powers within us: the power to withdraw, the power to pack up, the power to tolerate, the power to accommodate, the power of discernment, the power to judge, the power to face obstacles and the power to co-operate. As these powers develop, we begin to understand that we are much more than a physical body; we are a metaphysical energy that functions through our physical organs. And when we practise these eight powers every day, everyone benefits in the long-term because whatever actions we take impact on our surroundings and those around us.

This book will first open your eyes, making you aware of the twelve transformative values, and then it will help you to develop the eight personal powers, for only by practising them in your everyday life can you master them. Then you will have all the tools you need to hand to live a quality life and inspire others to do the same.

Dadi Janki, 2011

DAY 1

VALUE: FAITH

"Trust in others wins co-operation from them."

Contemplation

To have faith in others also means reinforcing other people's faith in themselves. This naturally increases their self-confidence and creates enthusiasm. Then they become better able to respond to positive feelings and access their full potential.

APPLICATION

If I notice that someone I work with is not co-operating with me, I need to check my own faith in that person. When I am able to appreciate them for their unique qualities, my faith in that person will grow. As my faith develops, so will their attitude toward me. Gradually, we become closer and are able to work together more easily.

DAY 2

VALUE: HUMILITY

"The more humble you are, the more successful you will be."

CONTEMPLATION

Humility provides us with the wings to fly. It gives us an enthusiasm based on inner truth and allows us to move forward easily. When there is no humility, we find ourselves being pulled back again and again by difficult situations we've created for ourselves.

APPLICATION

When I do something, I need to make sure that I am enjoying it and take the time to remind myself of the joy it gives me. This frees me from the desire for recognition or praise. Then I will find myself succeeding in any task I undertake, and others will appreciate my efforts.

DAY 3

VALUE: LOVE

"Only when you love yourself can you forgive yourself."

CONTEMPLATION

Love gives us the power to forgive. Just as it is easy to forgive a person we love, when we truly love ourselves, we will also be able to forgive ourselves. Only then will we find ourselves learning and progressing rather than holding on to past mistakes.

APPLICATION

When I notice myself making a mistake, I will remind myself that to progress in life I have to be able to forgive myself. I need to learn from my mistakes so that I do not repeat them.

DAY 4

VALUE: USING TIME WELL

"To be wise is to use the treasure of time well."

CONTEMPLATION

We are well aware of the physical resources we have and usually make good use of them. But we are often careless about the resource of time. We tend to believe that using time well means planning the day and working according to that plan – and we manage to do that most of the time. But all of us find that a large amount of time goes to waste.

APPLICATION

Using time well means being aware of where I am investing it. When I invest time in creating positive thoughts, words and actions, then I save lots of time. And I am sure to get the best out of this investment, too – I find myself gaining good returns from everything that I do.

DAY 5

VALUE: TRUTH

"Truth brings simplicity."

CONTEMPLATION

When we understand the power of truth, life becomes simple. Falsehood only leads to artificiality and complications. If we have the power of truth within us and live with it, then we will never want to show off, nor become dependent on the compliments of others. Then life becomes easy.

APPLICATION

If I ever find myself having negative thoughts because of my expectations of others, I should ask myself what I expect from them that I do not have within myself. The more I learn the art of connecting to my own innate truth, the easier it will be to keep my life free from complications.

DAY 6

VALUE: GIVING

"To recognize others' needs and to give unconditionally is to be truly happy."

CONTEMPLATION

We expect a great deal from others and often forget what we have to offer them in return. We find it difficult to give of ourselves unconditionally, and instead tend to think about what we are going to get out of giving. By focusing on what we hope to gain, we lose the joy of giving, and when we don't get what we expected experience negative feelings.

APPLICATION

There is true joy in giving. When I realize I am able to help someone, I will give them what they need without expecting anything in return. I will learn the pleasure of giving unconditionally, using my gifts to benefit others. This will put me get in touch with my inner self and help me experience true happiness.

DAY 7

VALUE: CO-OPERATION

"Every task is easy for the one who is able to co-operate."

CONTEMPLATION

Often, we prefer to do everything alone. We feel that it is easier not to involve too many people in order to avoid conflict with different personalities. The responsibility of co-operating may even feel like a burden weighing us down.

APPLICATION

Working together is the best way to achieve success. I need to recognize that everyone has his or her individual talents, and when I am able to connect with them, we can work together to complete the task. Even the biggest project becomes easy when everyone co-operates. My positive feelings combined with the good wishes of everyone involved will help us succeed.

DAY 8

VALUE: RESPECT

"To respect other people is to understand and appreciate their unique qualities."

CONTEMPLATION

We expect others to change to fit in with our own expectations and values. Yet often we find that nothing changes in the way we want it to. This creates irritation and discontentment.

APPLICATION

I need to understand that every person around me is different; everyone is unique and has amazing qualities and talents. When I look at others in this way I no longer expect them to change according to my wishes, but instead find that I respect them for who they are.

DAY 9

VALUE: SELF-CONTROL

"Control over oneself is the only real control."

CONTEMPLATION

Normally we understand control as something we need to have over others or situations. So when things go wrong, our first thought is to exert control. But since neither the situations nor the people can ever be in our hands, we are unable to succeed in controlling them.

APPLICATION

Instead of trying to control things that are out of my hands, I need to learn how to control myself. By being aware of my own actions and reactions, I can learn self-control. This will affect how I behave when things go wrong, allowing me to approach events and people in a more positive, constructive way.

DAY 10

VALUE: TRUTH

"Truth never needs to be proved."

CONTEMPLATION

Truth is always revealed in the right place, at the right moment. We don't need to be concerned about proving it. We need only be concerned with being it and living it. Trying to prove truth reveals stubbornness, and is often counterproductive.

APPLICATION

When someone does not believe what I say, I need to ask myself whether I truly believe in it. If I am sure it is true, then I need not be concerned about proving it to others. Only when I doubt something will I wish to prove it to everyone.

DAY 11

VALUE: LOVE

"The one who is full of love is always happy."

CONTEMPLATION

When we are full of love for everyone, there is no space for negativity. This unselfish love means that we have only positive thoughts and experience constant happiness.

APPLICATION

Today, I'll start the day by thinking of all the people I will come into contact with. Then I will think about having love for all of them. This thought will help me throughout the day. I will find myself accepting others as they are and extending good wishes to them.

DAY 12

VALUE: FAITH

"To think 'I can win' is to ensure victory."

CONTEMPLATION

We tend to attribute success to the resources available or the help of those around us. But in spite of our best efforts, we sometimes find ourselves failing. We might blame this on bad luck or a negative event.

APPLICATION

Today I will notice how my successes are not so much based on what I have as on what I do with what I have. When I believe that I can win, I will win.

DAY 13

VALUE: POSITIVITY

"To see things as they are is to be free from negativity."

CONTEMPLATION

We don't usually see things as they are, but as we are. We tend to color what we see according to our past experiences and our attitudes and beliefs. When our experiences of the past are negative, we tend to become negative too. This is why some situations tend to bring about sorrow and unhappy feelings.

APPLICATION

Every situation contains something bright and beautiful. When I make an attempt to see things for what they are, I am able to see this positive aspect. Then I am able to let go of the negativity associated with past experiences and appreciate what exists in the present.

DAY 14

VALUE: TRUTH

"If you are always truthful, you will have nothing to fear."

CONTEMPLATION

True courage comes when we acknowledge the power of truth within. If we are constantly truthful, we will have nothing to fear. The power of truth will give us the courage to meet the challenges we face every day.

APPLICATION

I must make sure that my actions are based on truth. Then if things go wrong, I will be able to maintain courage. If I keep reminding myself that I have the power of truth within me, I will be able to overcome whatever challenges come my way.

DAY 15

VALUE: FOCUS

"The one whose keeps their destination in focus will be successful."

CONTEMPLATION

As we travel toward our destination, it's easy to get distracted. We sometimes become so busy thinking about the little things that affect our lives that we lose focus and stop moving forward.

APPLICATION

First, I need to clarify my goal, then think about how I'm going to work toward it. When situations arise to distract me I need to remind myself that they are only sideshows; they are not important. Instead, to find success, I need to keep my energies focused on my destination.

DAY 16

VALUE: POSITIVITY

"To remain cheerful is to simplify all problems."

CONTEMPLATION

When faced with problems it seems difficult to maintain inner cheer – the mind is caught up with more and more negativity, fear and worry. This, makes problems seem bigger than they are and stops us finding solutions and working constructively to solve issues.

APPLICATION

When I recognize a problem, the first thing I need to do is to smile. When I am happy within myself and understand that every situation has something to teach me, I will find solutions more quickly and easily.

DAY 17

VALUE: DISCERNMENT

"To see things as they are is to be free from the influence of weaknesses."

CONTEMPLATION

Sometimes we react to small situations. Our feelings are dependent on the situations we face. If we experience negative feelings, we often try to change them. But this can be difficult, either because of our personality, the personality trait we are working with at the time, or a particularly challenging event.

APPLICATION

To change my reactions to the different situations that face me, I need to change the way I see things. I need to understand the situation as it is and not let it be colored by my personality traits. When I see things as they are, I can control how I act in situations instead of simply reacting.

DAY 18

VALUE: SIMPLICITY

"To be simple is to become an example."

CONTEMPLATION

Simplicity is often mistaken as ordinariness. It is sometimes associated with lack of color and variety. So we rarely focus on simplicity in our words and actions. Instead, we tend to add as much color as we can in order to seem more attractive or impressive. In the process we move ourselves away from our original nature.

APPLICATION

To be simple is to think of myself as like a seed, which is complete, yet simple. True simplicity means discovering and using the qualities within me. It means becoming closer to my true nature and being. Once I allow these qualities to flow out from my inner self, others are able to take inspiration from me. With my own simplicity I will become an example for others.

DAY 19

VALUE: TRUTH

"Where there is truth there is victory."

CONTEMPLATION

There is a saying that goes, "The boat of truth may rock, but it will never sink." When we are truthful we might experience some setbacks or dissatisfaction, but will ultimately attain victory.

APPLICATION

When I am going through difficult times, I must remind myself that the truth within me will eventually lead to victory. This faith will help me to approach every situation with a positive attitude.

DAY 20

VALUE: HUMILITY

"Where there is humility, there is benefit to many."

CONTEMPLATION

Just as the tree laden with fruit bows down, so does one who is humble. A humble person brings benefit to all those around. Humility helps us give in all situations, and makes it easy for others to take what we have to offer.

APPLICATION

In all my interactions with others, it is more important to see what I can give, than to expect anything. Then, even when I face criticism, I will have no problems. Humility helps me to bow easily.

DAY 21

VALUE: POSITIVITY

"To be free from negative thoughts gives the ability to fly."

CONTEMPLATION

When difficult situations come our way, we tend to fill the mind with negativity, which drains us of energy. It is easy to become overwhelmed, leaving no space for constructive thinking.

APPLICATION

When I encounter a difficult situation, I need to try not to get caught up with why it happened or dwell on the problems. Instead, I need to realize that I am stronger than the situation and am able to overcome it. Once I start thinking about how to solve the problem, I'll find a way to fly above it.

DAY 22

VALUE: LOVE

"Love provides the environment for everyone's growth."

CONTEMPLATION

Normally, in a relationship we expect things from those we get close to. We feel that because we love them we have rights over them. Because of our expectations we are not able to give the other person freedom to move forward or progress.

APPLICATION

When I experience true love I can provide the right environment for people so that they can progress in their lives. Today I will not hold onto those I love nor expect them to do everything according to my needs, but instead will give them real support.

DAY 23

VALUE: TRUTH

"The one who is truthful is loved and trusted by all."

CONTEMPLATION

When we are truthful, our words and actions become equal. We do what we say and say what we do. Because of this we will be well regarded and loved by everyone.

APPLICATION

Today, I will take up one thing I have not been able to fulfill and believe I will do it. I need to remind myself that I have the power of truth within me and that it makes my words and actions equal.

DAY 24

VALUE: BEING PRESENT

"To understand the importance of my actions is to create a fortune for myself."

CONTEMPLATION

We usually blame fortune when something goes wrong. We complain that life is unfair, or regret past actions that have brought about the current situation. But to dwell on what went wrong in the past means that we cannot fully experiencing the present.

APPLICATION

Instead of cursing my past actions, I need to make the most of the present. Whatever I do today, will benefit me now, as well as in the future. I need to pay attention so that I take the right action and create the best fortune for myself.

Day 25

Value: Serving others

"The will to serve others creates opportunity."

Contemplation

We often want to help others or serve them in some way, but find that the right opportunity never arrives. At other times, we find the opportunity given to us isn't the one we wanted – it doesn't match our desires.

Application

I need to be constantly thinking about how I can help others. I won't wait for better situations or opportunities to come up. Instead I will help others whenever I can. Providing help in little ways will give me the opportunity to serve in bigger ways.

DAY 26

VALUE: ENTHUSIASM

"To be enthusiastic is to be free."

CONTEMPLATION

When everything is going well, it's easy to be enthusiastic and interested in moving forward. But when even a little thing goes wrong, we tend to lose all enthusiasm to do anything. This makes us feel tied down and then it becomes difficult or even impossible to put in enough effort to move forward.

APPLICATION

A caged bird has the ability to fly, but is unable to spread its wings and soar. I need to remind myself that being enthusiastic in all situations is like being free bird reaching great heights. When I can experience this inner freedom and appreciate the joy it brings, I will be able to sustain it even when things go wrong.

DAY 27

VALUE: TRUTH

"The power of truth will enable you to learn from your mistakes."

CONTEMPLATION

The power of truth within equips us to learn from all situations. When things go wrong we are able to reflect on how to learn from mistakes rather than making excuses to others and ourselves. Making excuses means hiding from the truth and stops us from learning and progressing.

APPLICATION

Thinking about something that went wrong today, I need to ask myself about my part in the situation. When I understand this, I will know how to correct myself in the future.

DAY 28

VALUE: HONESTY

"Honesty brings progress."

CONTEMPLATION

Honesty is usually associated with telling the truth or being open with others. We often find it easier to be honest with others than with ourselves. It can be difficult to admit our weaknesses, even to ourselves. But in order to progress, we need to be brave enough to face the truth.

APPLICATION

More than anything else I need to be honest with myself. That means reflecting upon my thoughts, words and behavior. If I start making excuses for myself, I am not being truly honest. When I become aware of my weaknesses, I will be able to address them and move forward.

DAY 29

VALUE: USING OUR GIFTS

"To be special is to bring love and beauty to every word and every act."

CONTEMPLATION

Sometimes we hold back, waiting for the right situation to use our gifts. But there are often times when we could have done more. Each of us has the power to turn ordinary moments into memorable ones.

APPLICATION

When I am aware of my own gifts in a conscious way, I can make everything I say or do meaningful and powerful. Nothing is wasted, or even ordinary; everything I do becomes special. I am not caught up with the ordinariness or the negativity of a situation, but am able to enjoy the moment by making it my own.

Day 30

Value: Giving

"To consider oneself to be big is to have a generous heart."

Contemplation

When we consider ourselves 'big', we usually expect the same from others. We want them to give us respect and obey us. But we do not always find others listening to us or obeying us. This leads to disappointment and the urge to use our authority in a more forceful way.

Application

To be big means being a giver. If I am big, I need to understand that there are others less fortunate than myself, and I need to use what I have been given to help them. This attitude will help me attract others' good wishes, which in turn will help me progress.

DAY 31

VALUE: SELF-RESPECT

"To transform the ordinary into something special is to be truly fortunate."

CONTEMPLATION

Fortune is usually perceived as having a chance to be in a special place or to do special things. Life reveals that we cannot always be in such a position nor do we always get the chance to do special things. At such times we may consider ourselves less fortunate.

APPLICATION

When I respect myself and acknowledge the strengths and talents that make me unique, I connect with my inner self. I realize I have the power within me to make everything I do – even the most ordinary act – special. Then I become truly fortunate.

DAY 32

VALUE: LOVE

"The one way to change others is to deal with them with love."

CONTEMPLATION

When we love others, you have good wishes for them. We want to help them change for their own good rather than for our benefit. Others quickly respond to this unselfish love and we see them changing.

APPLICATION

Today I'll think of one person I want to help change. Before I think of changing that person I need to think about all the love I have for him or her. I also need to make sure that the change I want in the other person is intended for his or her own good and not motivated by my own selfish reasons.

DAY 33

VALUE: HUMILITY

"Humility equips people to realize their mistakes and correct themselves."

CONTEMPLATION

Real humility reflects a truth that doesn't need to be expressed in words. The power of our inner state of being will make the other person realize the error of their ways.

APPLICATION

When I direct or question someone, I need to be aware of my attitude and remind myself of the humility within – only then should I say what I have to say. When inspired by humility, my words will be for the other person's benefit and will enable him or her to learn.

DAY 34

VALUE: SELFLESSNESS

"Selflessness brings happiness."

CONTEMPLATION

Selfishness is always accompanied by a desire, and because of this desire there can never be satisfaction. We always want something more. Someone who cannot overcome his or her own desires will never become a giver. If we lack the ability to share resources for others' benefit, we can never be happy.

APPLICATION

When I am selfless I have respect for my own abilities, and I am able to use them for the benefit of others. Because I have the satisfaction of using my talents, I am not looking for others to appreciate me. I become a giver instead of a taker, which brings me happiness and good wishes from others.

DAY 35

VALUE: NON-VIOLENCE

"True non-violence means never hurting others even through words."

CONTEMPLATION

Most of us make a great effort not to hurt people physically, but sometimes we hurt others through our words, often accidently.

APPLICATION

Today I will really think about the consequence of my words before I speak and consider how they might hurt others. I will also notice how when I do express negativity it makes those around me feel negative, which in turn affects me for the worst too.

Day 36

Value: Humility

"True humility comes from self-respect."

Contemplation

When we respect ourselves, we are able to remain humble in every situation. When we lack self-respect, any comments or criticism hurt the ego and we tend to lose our humility.

Application

When I find myself getting affected by criticism, I need to check whether I am sure of what I'm doing. I need to look within and learn to appreciate my own special qualities, and think about how I can use them my daily life. As my confidence grows, I will become humble.

Day 37

Value: Love

"Where there is love, the hardest task becomes easy to perform."

Contemplation

If something is difficult, it means there is no love attached to it. Where there is love, even a task as weighty a mountain becomes as light as cotton wool. Love makes work easier and lighter.

Application

Today is the day to love my work. Whatever I am doing, I must remember that I love my work. I will experiment with one thing that I have been finding difficult, reminding myself that I love it, and that is the reason why I am doing it.

DAY 38

VALUE: FORGIVENESS

"To let go of the past is to stop it having a negative impact on the present."

CONTEMPLATION

We are often slaves of the past. Even though something may have happened a long time ago, we often find ourselves unable to forgive and forget. We relive the negative feelings associated with it and find it hard to break free.

APPLICATION

I need to free my mind of the past. I need to reflect on what I have learnt from a past situation and learn to let go. But I can only forget the past when I am able to forgive others and myself; I can only forgive when I learn from what happened. When I learn from a situation, I free myself from the chains of the past.

DAY 39

VALUE: APPRECIATION

"To appreciate one's resources is to experience constant progress."

CONTEMPLATION

It is much easier to notice what we don't have than appreciate what we do. Whenever challenging situations come our way, we tend to focus on what we lack. With this attitude, we are unable to make an effort to change the situation. We then tend to blame others or make excuses.

APPLICATION

In challenging situations I need to make a special effort to appreciate and use what I have. When I continue to make effort in this way, every challenge will allow me to discover and use my hidden resources, making me richer. This will equip me to experience constant progress.

DAY 40

VALUE: FAITH

"The difference between the impossible and the possible lies in a person's determination."

CONTEMPLATION

When we start doing a new task, of course we believe we can achieve it. But sometimes as we move through that new project, we lose faith and courage and tend to give up mid-task. Difficulties and challenges cause our determination to waver and we become unable to achieve what we set out to do.

APPLICATION

What I require for achieving even the most impossible task is determination. When I am determined to succeed, I will not let anything get in my way and will move forward until I reach my destination. When I have faith in myself I will find that help comes my way and life is enriched by new experiences.

DAY 41

VALUE: RESPONSIBILITY

"Responsibility is best fulfilled with lightness."

CONTEMPLATION

Sometimes we become overwhelmed by our responsibilities which leads us into negative thinking. Our responsibilities weigh heavily on us, and we find ourselves wishing to escape. We need to learn how to carry responsibilities lightly in order to fulfill them.

APPLICATION

I need to think of my responsibilities not as burdens, but gifts. Becoming responsible for something helps me focus on doing the best I can for the benefit of others. In the process, I find I learn new skills, and my inner qualities develop as I learn. As a result, I will find myself enjoying what I am doing. My responsibilities no longer hold me back; they allow me to grow.

DAY 42

VALUE: POSITIVITY

"To recognize our own talents is to deserve life's best things."

CONTEMPLATION

We have many desires and expectations of life. When we don't get what we want, it can lead to negative feelings such as frustration, depression or a sense of inferiority. Sometimes we get so caught up in these feelings that good things become hidden from our vision.

APPLICATION

When I am aware of my own unique talents and how I use them, I become more able to recognize what I deserve rather than what I desire. I no longer focus on what I lack, but instead on the gifts I have been given, and how I can to use my resources to attain what I desire.

DAY 43

VALUE: LOVE

"The one who loves is the one who gives."

CONTEMPLATION

True love is free from expectations. When we discover the love within we can endlessly give it away. Whether another person gives back or not, true love enables us to continue giving unselfishly.

APPLICATION

Let today be the day I discover the love within me and share it with others. I will make sure I carry out at least one act that shows my love of the people in my life, and feel the love flowing from within me out to those around me.

Day 44

Value: Happiness

"To celebrate is to have constant happiness."

Contemplation

At special times, we tend to come under the influence of the festivity and enjoy the beauty of the time. But as time passes, situations change and we become unable to maintain that same state of happiness – we lose our zeal and enthusiasm. Then, we long for something to happen to change our mood.

Application

I need to be the master of the situation rather than its victim. It is good to benefit from the beauty of the present, but not to be dependent on it. Whatever happiness celebrations bring, I need to sustain my own inner happiness. This is true celebration and brings me new happiness with each step.

DAY 45

VALUE: INTROSPECTION

"Attention relieves one from tension."

CONTEMPLATION

We sometimes feel stressed by the responsibilities we take on. We find it difficult to relieve ourselves of tension, especially when we feel the demand of situations or expectations beyond our capabilities.

APPLICATION

Especially in demanding situations, but in general life, too, the way to relieve tension is to have constant attention. It is important to focus attention on myself during difficult times, but it is also important during normal conditions. Attention makes me check and change myself, and this relieves tension.

DAY 46

VALUE: RESPECT

"To give respect is to receive respect."

CONTEMPLATION

We normally expect respect from others and when others don't behave according to our expectations, tend to get disappointed. We only think about what else others have to give – but things always don't go according to expectations.

APPLICATION

Instead of expecting others to change according to my wishes and instead of expecting others' respect, I need to notice whether I give respect back. The more I accept and respect people for what they are, the more my mind will be at peace (free from wasteful and negative thoughts). People will then start responding to my feelings and give me respect too.

DAY 47

VALUE: PEACE

"To be an embodiment of peace is to be bestow peace"

CONTEMPLATION

People in the world only want peace and happiness. When we experience peace ourselves, we become able to give others this experience. Where there is peace, happiness naturally follows.

APPLICATION

I need to spend a few moments alone each day. During this time I should practise stabilizing myself with one powerful thought and allow the experience of peace from within to flow out to others. When I meet people, my inner peace helps keep my mind free from negative thoughts, and I will find that others are free from them too.

DAY 48

VALUE: TOLERANCE

"The power of truth gives us the ability to tolerate."

CONTEMPLATION

When someone disbelieves us, we tend to argue back and try to prove our point. In spite of our great efforts, we are not usually able to convince them. We should consider the simple fact that the more we talk, the less we are listened to. This means we end up feeling more frustrated.

APPLICATION

When someone challenges the truth of my words, I need to think about whether there is something I can correct or learn. When I start to do this, instead of being stubborn about what I have to say or blaming others, I will find it easier to be tolerant.

Day 49

Value: Hope

"To give someone hope is to help them overcome their weaknesses."

Contemplation

When we notice someone making mistakes, we tend to react to those mistakes and draw attention to them. We go on talking about the issue until the other person realizes his or her mistake. But the other person rarely benefits from such an approach. Either they lack the courage to accept their mistakes, or they do not want to change.

Application

When I recognize someone's mistake, I need to make sure I handle it in the way that will benefit him or her most. By focusing on their positive qualities, I make sure they do not become disheartened, and instead feel inspired to make a change within themselves.

DAY 50

VALUE: DETERMINATION

"Success is achieved through accurate efforts."

CONTEMPLATION

We tend to associate success with what we get, rather than how much effort we put in. So when things don't turn out the way we expect, we associate negative feelings with the lack of success. Then we stop putting in further effort.

APPLICATION

If I put in accurate efforts to succeed at a task, I try to do my best. Because of this contribution, others will help, contributing whatever they can to bring the project to fruition. Success follows. When I do the right thing, I will experience constant self-progress, even if the result is not what I expected.

DAY 51

VALUE: ENTHUSIASM

"To be free from carelessness is to be constantly enthusiastic."

CONTEMPLATION

When we see others being careless in their work, we tend to become careless too. We think that since the others have allowed weaknesses to take hold, it is acceptable for us to do the same. Such carelessness prevents us from being enthusiastic and making effort to improve.

APPLICATION

Carelessness has a tendency to spread from one person to another. When I see someone working carelessly, I need to remain strong within myself and pay close attention to my work. This will help me to move ahead with enthusiasm.

Day 52

Value: Positivity

"To see positivity in the self is to move toward inner perfection."

Contemplation

Whenever we make a mistake – or are not able to keep pace with the challenges that come our way – we tend to see our negative aspects. The reminder of these negative aspects strengthens them and we find ourselves using them over and again.

Application

Instead of focusing on my negative qualities, today I need to pay more attention to my positive qualities. The more I use these positive qualities in a conscious way, the more these qualities will begin to be visible in my life.

Day 53

Value: Sweetness

"The nectar of sweetness spreads happiness and increases success."

Contemplation

When a big task has to be accomplished – especially under pressure – we tend to become task-oriented. We only focus on the task at hand and don't give the same attention to our relationships at work. This prevents us from increasing work-efficiency.

Application

I need to pay special attention to maintaining my relationships as I get my work done. Discovering my own specialties and what I can contribute when I work with others spreads sweetness. This sweetness within spreads positive vibrations and creates a happy, productive environment, which in turn leads us all to greater success.

DAY 54

VALUE: RESPECT

"To be blind to the weakness of others is to be rich."

CONTEMPLATION

We tend to be sensitive to the weaknesses of others. We immediately see them, which affects our attitude toward others and colors our interactions. We find it difficult to see anything but those weaknesses.

APPLICATION

The solution lies in becoming aware of everyone's unique gifts. The more I am able to do this, the more I will encourage another person to use what they have been given for the benefit of all. I will gradually find that I can transform my relationships with others and experience richness and newness through every experience.

Day 55

Value: Stability

"Difficulties and setbacks bring forth hidden treasure within."

Contemplation

When we are faced with difficult situations, we may feel that we either lack the resources we need, or that are not able to make best use of them. Then, as well as experiencing much negativity, we are unable to make real progress.

Application

When I master the art of remaining stable even in the most negative situations, I learn how to use the treasures hidden within me. My mind is no longer disturbed by negative thoughts and I find it easy to face and learn from each situation as it arrives.

DAY 56

VALUE: POSITIVITY

"The one who is moldable is real gold."

CONTEMPLATION

We are often easily influenced by the negativity in the world. Every incident and interaction has an impact, and we find ourselves absorbing a great deal of impurity from outside. This is like mixing alloy with gold; when we are colored with negativity within, we are unable to be easily molded. And when we are unable to change, we are unable to grow.

APPLICATION

I need to keep myself free from the negativity of outside situations and other people. The best way to do this is to develop my inner positivity. It is like building a strong defense system against negative thoughts. When I am able to maintain inner purity and positivity, I find myself moldable again.

DAY 57

VALUE: LOVE

"To do a task with love is to be consistently successful."

CONTEMPLATION

When we start something new, we usually do well to start with, but success doesn't last. This often happens when we do something because we have to. When we are made to act by external forces, we're unlikely to work hard at the task for long.

APPLICATION

Love brings consistent success; once I've experienced the joy of the task itself, I'll never give up. If I am doing something I love, I will put all my energy into making it work and doing the best I can.

DAY 58

VALUE: RESPONSIBILITY

"Accepting responsibility means accepting challenge."

CONTEMPLATION

In many situations life brings our way we have two choices – either we meet them bravely and take responsibility for our lives and the choices we make, or we try to escape. The second option brings neither external success nor inner satisfaction.

APPLICATION

Inner satisfaction lies in accepting challenges rather than trying to escape them. I need to remain on the field in the game of life instead of just being a spectator. The more I play, the more expertise I gain. Keeping this thought in mind enables me to accept all the challenges life brings.

DAY 59

VALUE: BEING PRESENT

"To celebrate is to enjoy every moment."

CONTEMPLATION

Normally when we celebrate, we forget our worries for a time and enjoy those around us. But once the celebration is over, we return to routine thoughts. Regarding celebration as something temporary means we often don't get as much enjoyment from life as we could.

APPLICATION

Real celebration means enjoying the beauty and joy of each and every moment. By celebrating every moment, I will be constantly enthusiastic. I will stop looking for special occasions to be happy but instead will make the best use of every moment.

DAY 60

VALUE: STABILITY

"To achieve success, we must first develop inner stability."

CONTEMPLATION

When a situation is good, our state of mind is good too. But when something challenging happens, we experience fear or anxiety. It is not so much that the situation goes wrong, it is more that our reaction goes wrong.

APPLICATION

In order to experience success or to feel victorious, I need to change the way I respond to situations. Even in the most negative situations today I need to remind myself that even if the situation itself is not in my hands – how I choose to respond to it surely is. Then I will make the best choices.

Day 61

Value: Openness

"Openness to learning brings progress."

Contemplation

When someone corrects us or offers advice, we often meet them with resistance and become unwilling to listen. If we put in a lot of effort, we may not be able to listen to others' suggestions. This kind of attitude does not help us to learn and progress.

Application

I need to keep my mind constantly open to learning in order to experience constant progress. When I have this attitude I learn from everything that happens. Then I will be able to improve in each and every task.

DAY 62

VALUE: ENTHUSIASM

"The one who is constantly full of enthusiasm inspires others."

CONTEMPLATION

Whenever problems come our way, we tend to feel weighed down by negative thoughts. Heaviness in the mind prevents us from moving forward with enthusiasm and makes it tricky for us to inspire others.

APPLICATION

Whenever I encounter a difficult situation, I need to make a special effort to remain free and light. The more enthusiastic I am, the more progress I will make. My attitude will inspire others, too.

DAY 63

VALUE: FAITH

"To be free from worry is to find the right solutions."

CONTEMPLATION

Whenever we are faced with a problem, we naturally begin to
worry. This worry leads to a mass of negative thoughts. The
mind becomes so consumed with them that we can't find the
solution, nor can we stop worrying.

APPLICATION

The only way to find a solution is to keep my mind free from
worry. To do this, I need to have the faith that there is a
solution and that I will find it. Keeping my mind free in this
way switches on my intuition so that I automatically become
able to make the right decision.

DAY 64

VALUE: HUMILITY

"Truth is proved when it is combined with humility."

CONTEMPLATION

When we think we know the truth and are truthful, we can become convinced we are right. We are not able to see what the other person has to say and continue to put forth our own perspective. This can lead to futile arguments and conflict.

APPLICATION

With truth, I also need humility. Humility helps me to put forth my ideas to another person in a detached way. The truth within me will help me understand the other person and will keep me open to his or her point of view. I will get my point across without much difficulty because the other person will also be able to see my point of view.

DAY 65

VALUE: LEARNING FROM MISTAKES

"Being careful brings progress."

CONTEMPLATION

When we make mistakes, we sometimes try to justify them. We give excuses and compare ourselves with others who have made similar mistakes. But we fail to learn from our mistakes, and often repeat them. Then we are unable to experience the joy of true progress.

APPLICATION

True wisdom lies in learning from others' mistakes. When someone makes a mistake, I become richer from the experience. I need not go through the same experience myself to learn from it. When I am constantly aware of other people's actions, I experience progress at every step.

DAY 66

VALUE: UNDERSTANDING

"To see things as they are is to be free from the influence of weaknesses."

CONTEMPLATION

Our feelings are colored by the situations we face. We might try to change negative feelings as they arise, but sometimes are prevented from doing so by our personality as a whole or the personality trait we are working with at that time.

APPLICATION

I need to change my vision – the way I see things. I need to understand the situation as it is and not let it be colored by my personality traits. When I see things as they are, I become better able to act in situations instead of just reacting.

Day 67

Value: Self-Respect

"To value one's own part is to play it well."

Contemplation

We often compare ourselves to other people – their qualities, status in life or possessions. But this is not always helpful. We do not see the whole picture, and often feel as if we are lacking in some way. This prevents us from appreciating our own qualities.

Application

It is important to understand the uniqueness of my own role in life, to accept it and to put in effort to play it well. When I do this, I start to appreciate the purpose of my role on life's stage and use my unique gifts in an appropriate way.

DAY 68

VALUE: LEARNING LESSONS

"To have learnt means bringing about a practical change."

CONTEMPLATION

From every situation we absorb important lessons. But sometimes we find ourselves making the same mistakes again and again. Although we have understood the lesson, we are unable to bring about real change.

APPLICATION

Once I realize and learn from a mistake, I need to spend time mulling it over. I need to ensure I don't ever repeat the mistake. This will help me bring about real change.

Day 69

Value: Introspection

"To be free from weaknesses is to move forward constantly."

Contemplation

Most of the time we manage to win over our weaknesses and progress forward, but sometimes we are defeated by our own weaknesses and experience failure. Then instead of progressing, we find ourselves moving backward.

Application

In order to benefit others and myself, I should recognize and remove the last traces of weakness within me. To do that I need to constantly check the cause of the weakness and remove it. Such checking and changing helps me to overcome my weaknesses.

Day 70

Value: Using time well

"Those who understand the importance of time make full use of it."

Contemplation

We have a tendency to postpone things to the last moment. So when we need to finish a job and unforeseen things crop up, we often feel pressurized. Then we stop being able to work well and begin to wish we had more time.

Application

I need to understand the importance of time and do jobs immediately. Today I'll think about how if I lose this moment, there is no chance of getting it back. If I use the time at hand fruitfully, I'll always remain light and available to work on things that arise suddenly.

DAY 71

VALUE: HONESTY

"Honesty provides the solution to problems."

CONTEMPLATION

If our reaction to problems or people is to give up or run away, we are deceiving ourselves. We will not be able to avoid the situation by going elsewhere; this merely puts it off. If we try to run away from problems rather than dealing with them we will find ourselves experiencing the same difficulties repeatedly.

APPLICATION

Instead of trying to change a situation, I need to be honest with myself and address the weakness within me that is causing the problem. Once I am aware of it, I can work to change it, and will be able to overcome problems in the future.

DAY 72

VALUE: CHANGE

"Change is necessary for growth."

CONTEMPLATION

We usually recognize when we need to bring about change in ourselves – we tend to feel a strong desire to change. But it is much more difficult to turn this understanding and desire into practical action.

APPLICATION

As soon as I understand that I need to change, I have to work at bringing that change about. I need to tell myself that there is no better time than now.

DAY 73

VALUE: CALMNESS

"To maintain an inner state of calm is to arrive at the right solutions."

CONTEMPLATION

When we confront a problem or a difficult situation, we tend to face it with worry or negative thoughts. Although outwardly we might seem to face the situation, we are not able to deal with it. And most of the time we find that we are failing.

APPLICATION

The best way to deal with a situation is to start by calming the mind. Only a calm mind can find the answers to problems. I need to understand that every problem has an answer. When my mind is relaxed I can trust my intuition to find the answer that is already there.

DAY 74

VALUE: TIRELESSNESS

"Tirelessness is never having the feeling of being washed out."

CONTEMPLATION

Tirelessness is not just the capacity of the body; it has more to do with the ability of the spirit. Tirelessness means not allowing anything to take away the color and beauty of life. It comes from an appreciation of the variety that life brings, which enables us to be stable in all situations.

APPLICATION

Even in difficult situations, I need to remind myself that I can enjoy the beauty of life. I need to enjoy learning from my failures as much as I enjoy success. This will allow me to move on, and I will find I have more energy in difficult circumstances.

Day 75

Value: Faith

"To be free from worry is to find the right solutions."

Contemplation

When faced with a problem, it's quite natural to worry. But the worry creates a great number of wasteful thoughts. We can't find the solution, but neither can we stop worrying. A worried mind filled with negative thoughts will never find the right solution.

Application

The only way to find a solution is to keep my mind free from worry. To do this I need first to have the faith that there is a solution and that I will find it.

DAY 76

VALUE: SHARING

"True joy lies in sharing things with others."

CONTEMPLATION

When we consider sharing, we sometimes wonder if it is really beneficial. Often people believe that when we share, we find ourselves a little poorer as a result. If we believe that only the person we share with benefits, we will find it difficult to share our time and resources.

APPLICATION

When we share our inner resources, we reap the benefit. Every time we give, we not only get back from others but also experience that quality ourselves. When we share our physical resources, it is our own experience which is important rather than the outcome. The experience of sharing will inspire others to share with us.

DAY 77

VALUE: LISTENING

"The power to listen brings inner peace."

CONTEMPLATION

Sometimes when someone says something, there is a tendency to feel hurt even if the other person did not mean to be hurtful. This is because we hear only the words without understanding their meaning. This leads to misunderstanding and conflict, and can spoil relationships.

APPLICATION

When someone tells me something, I need to listen to the person rather than merely hear his words. When I am understand the intentions behind the words I will be able to take something from them instead of creating conflict.

Day 78

Value: Calmness

"Calmness of mind brings accuracy in judgment."

Contemplation

When a challenge demands accurate judgment, we tend to become panicky. Many wasteful thoughts come to mind. The decisions we take in such a state of mind tend to go wrong.

Application

I need to guide my mind toward a state of calm before making a decision in challenging situations. In order to do this, I need a long period of practice – even when the situation demands that I speed up my activities. Training the mind over a long period of time helps it to stay calm even in challenging times.

DAY 79

VALUE: OPTIMISM

"Remaining cheerful simplifies all problems."

CONTEMPLATION

When faced with problems it can seem difficult to maintain inner cheer; the mind gets caught up with more and more negativity, fear or worry. Because of this, the problem seems bigger than it is and we lose the ability to find solutions and work constructively.

APPLICATION

The first step I need to take when I recognize a problem is to smile to myself. When I make sure I am happy within, I know that every situation will pass and has something to teach me. Then I will find solutions come more quickly and easily.

DAY 80

VALUE: INDEPENDENCE

"True help involves giving support in such a way that people become independent."

CONTEMPLATION

It is natural to want support others. But sometimes our good intentions go awry. By giving people too much help, we actually make them dependent on us and prevent them from learning on their own.

APPLICATION

I must remind myself that my aim in helping others is to make them independent and strong so that they are able to support others, too. My help should never make people weak.

DAY 81

VALUE: RESPONSIBILITY

"The way to be accurate is to be responsible at all times."

CONTEMPLATION

Very often we find ourselves leaving things to chance or to other people. We tend to take care of the big issues and become careless with little things. When we delegate tasks for others to take care of and they don't do them, we become disappointed.

APPLICATION

I must recognize that I am fully responsible for the task at hand – both the big things and the little items – then I'll never be careless. I'll make a point of taking care of every last aspect. This will make me more accurate and help me to delegate.

DAY 82

VALUE: LISTENING

"To listen well is to create harmonious relationships."

CONTEMPLATION

Taking the time to listen and understand others helps us to relate to them well. We need to be concerned not with what is visible, but what we see within them. This helps us to recognize others' needs and provide an environment in which they can grow.

APPLICATION

When I am open to the world of others, I am able to create harmonious relationships. I will not expect people to be like me, but have respect for what they are, understanding that we are all unique individuals with something special to offer. By recognizing and celebrating differences, all my relationships will grow stronger.

DAY 83

VALUE: BALANCE

"Being truly successful means balancing my desires with what is best for me."

CONTEMPLATION

Sometimes it is difficult to be successful because there is a mismatch between what we desire and what we want. Although on some level, we know what is best for us, we are unable to turn that knowledge into action.

APPLICATION

I need to put in conscious effort to work out what is best for me, and compare it to what I desire. When what I need matches what I desire I will find it easy to move forward and will find success.

Day 84

Value: Positivity

"Paying attention to thoughts increases their power."

Contemplation

We need to have a lot of positive thoughts to bring about a change in our lives. But most of the time we are not able to bring this into practice. As time passes, a thought loses its importance and we find ourselves caught up in negativity.

Application

I need to keep a chart of my wasteful and negative thoughts as well as my powerful and positive thoughts. Only when I am consciously aware of how much time I am wasting on negative thoughts will I be able to change. When I increase the number of positive thoughts, I increase my inner power.

DAY 85

VALUE: INTROSPECTION

"The one who pays attention to the self will constantly experience progress."

CONTEMPLATION

When faced with a situation, it is easy to think and talk about others and their mistakes. There is hardly any time to think about or understand ourselves and the mistakes we make. So we continue to repeat our mistakes again and again.

APPLICATION

Whatever situation I am faced with, I need to remind myself that I am the one who will benefit if I bring about a change in myself. With this thought in mind, I will be able to pay attention to my thoughts, words and actions in order to bring about positive change.

Day 86

Value: Freedom

"To be free from negativity is to be truly free."

Contemplation

All of us like freedom and we expect that others should give us
the opportunity to express ourselves as we like. But sometimes
this type of freedom is misused and we are unable to do the
right thing. Such actions based on false freedom harm all of us.

Application

True freedom means being totally free from negativity. When I
free myself from negative influences I will be able to take
responsibility for my actions. Then I automatically have the
freedom to do what I want because I will only use my freedom
to do things that benefit everyone.

DAY 87

VALUE: CONNECTING TO OTHERS

"The one who knows the art of connecting to others is successful."

CONTEMPLATION

We are normally kind to people who are good to us. But when someone is not behaving well, we tend to change our attitude, responses and behavior toward that person. We wait for the other person to change before changing ourselves. So we do not find change in others nor in ourselves.

APPLICATION

When I see others' inner qualities I connect to them more easily. I will not be dependent on another person's behavior for my own growth today. Instead, I will see each person's positive aspects and take them within myself. In this way I will become richer with each interaction.

DAY 88

VALUE: BALANCE

"To be balanced is to be successful in relationships."

CONTEMPLATION

To be balanced means doing the right thing at the right time. It is the ability to use the head and the heart simultaneously. It is the ability to enjoy love and discipline in equal measure.

APPLICATION

I will try to balance every act today and watch how this makes my relationships easier and brings me others' blessings. Then I will experience success in all I do and enjoy a life of bliss.

DAY 89

VALUE: TRUST

"Trust wins co-operation."

CONTEMPLATION

When we think we can do things without other people's help, it means that we have become arrogant or are unable to trust others. This lack of trust means we miss the chance to use others' potential for the benefit of the task in hand. We are deprived of a useful resource and will not achieve as much as we could by working together.

APPLICATION

I need to understand that co-operation can bring greater success. If I invest my time and resources in training and developing others' potential it will bring out the best in people. When they contribute more, or use their skills more effectively, we all achieve better results.

Day 90

Value: Wisdom

"The one who is wise is aware of the importance of nourishing the mind."

Contemplation

Every day we make time to nourish the body with food. We quickly become aware if we don't give it enough food – we become hungry. But we are not so aware of the spiritual food we require. If we are spiritually malnourished, our minds will be too weak to withstand attack from outside.

Application

Reading or listening to something good everyday will keep my mind healthy and happy. Thinking good thoughts over helps me to remember what I have heard. Then I become so healthy that when difficult situations come my way I have the inner strength to face them.

DAY 91

VALUE: DETERMINATION

"Linking promises with determination enables one to overcome all problems."

CONTEMPLATION

When we make a promise, we usually do so with a great deal of enthusiasm. We feel committed to fulfilling what we have said we will do. But if we face even a little opposition or difficulty in carrying out this promise, we tend to lose hope and often give up trying altogether.

APPLICATION

In order to bring about a change in me and fulfill my promise, I need to use the virtue of determination. When I find myself losing the enthusiasm to finish what I started, I need to remind myself of the importance of the promise I made. This will enable me to overcome the obstacles that stop me turning thoughts and words into action.

Day 92

Value: Understanding

"Working on building relationships brings understanding."

Contemplation

It's easy to speak negatively when we do not like something about someone. We often react without thinking, and become angry. Our words and behavior become negative or insulting. This further widens the gap and damages the relationship.

Application

When someone does something undesirable, I first need to try and understand the behavior. Every person has a reason to behave the way he or she does. If I can't understand it at the time, I need to think about what might have made them act in that way. The more I react to the other person and the bad behavior, the greater the distance between us. To mend the relationship, I need to remind myself of the other person's good qualities.

Day 93

Value: Determination

"Success is achieved through determined effort."

Contemplation

We tend to associate success with what we get, rather than how much effort we put in. So sometimes when things don't turn out the way we expected, we tend to think negatively because we feel unsuccessful. This discourages us from trying again.

Application

When I am determined to succeed, I will do my best. When others see how hard I'm working, they will help me and do whatever they can to help me achieve my goals. When I am determined to succeed, I develop and progress, even if the result is not what was expected.

DAY 94

VALUE: COMMUNICATION

"Lightness comes when words are accurate."

CONTEMPLATION

Sometimes it can be difficult to let others know how we feel. We use lots of words, but often find we haven't actually said much, or the other person hasn't understood our message. Then there is a tendency to use more words, which can make the situation worse, sometimes hurting others' feelings.

APPLICATION

If will try to use words accurately, then nothing more needs to be said. A few well-chosen words are sweet to hear, and do not hurt others. When my words are to the point, I feel light and free.

DAY 95

VALUE: ENTHUSIASM

"Being constantly enthusiastic helps others progress."

CONTEMPLATION

Problems can make us feel weighed down with negative thoughts. Heaviness of mind prevents us from moving forward with enthusiasm and then we find it difficult to help others progress.

APPLICATION

Whatever the circumstances I am faced with, I need to make special effort to maintain enthusiasm. Enthusiasm gives me courage, which helps me use my unique talents to benefit others. I will then begin to discover new resources within me, which can be used for everyone's benefit.

Day 96

Value: Positivity

"The power of stability can transform any situation."

Contemplation

Our first reaction to a difficult situation is often negative. There is a tendency to be carried away in a storm of negative thoughts. Such thoughts are of no use and lead us further from the solution.

Application

Thinking one positive thought everyday helps me to maintain stability. Constant practice will help me remain stable even in the most difficult circumstances. It enables me to prepare for any situation that comes my way, and equips me with the vigilance and tools I need to overcome difficulties.

DAY 97

VALUE: SELF-CONTROL

"Real control means having control over the self."

CONTEMPLATION

When we talk about control, we usually think about controlling others or situations. We rarely consider self-control – it sounds too difficult and painful. So it becomes tricky to change or adapt our thoughts, words and behavior and difficult to interest ourselves in self-control.

APPLICATION

To have control over myself means being a master. My thoughts, words and behavior need to be ruled by my orders. This is real self-control. To do this, I need to practise being a master and not to become a slave to anything. The more I practise the consciousness of being a master, the more everything that is mine will naturally obey my orders.

DAY 98

VALUE: FULFILLING PROMISES

"To make my promise practical brings benefit at each step."

CONTEMPLATION

We often make promises to ourselves and others. Although we are sincere at the time, the promise never actually gets fulfilled. The promise is wasted when we do not translate intentions into action.

APPLICATION

When I make a promise to bring about a change in myself I need to act immediately, making a practical plan that will help me turn the promise into reality. I also need to make sure I understand why fulfilling that promise is important for me. I need to keep reminding myself of what I have committed to do until I accomplish it.

DAY 99

VALUE: LOVE

"Words filled with good wishes bring change in others."

CONTEMPLATION

When we correct people, we often find that our words have little effect. We are so caught up with our own expectations that we fail to understand the other person. Then we don't get what we want, and the relationship can become strained.

APPLICATION

When I combine good wishes with the words I speak, love emerges. Whatever is spoken with love is free from selfishness and negativity and has a powerful effect on others. Only words spoken out of love can bring about a change in others – and in myself.

DAY 100

VALUE: LIGHTNESS

"To consider problems to be a game is to move forward with lightness."

CONTEMPLATION

People consider challenging situations to be problems we need to be rid of. We often avoid the situation or the people involved and we wish that everything would change. After the challenge has passed, we tend to feel drained.

APPLICATION

If I understand that problems are just a game, I will be able to play whatever part I have to. Then even when the most difficult problem comes my way, I can give my best because I understand the significance of what is happening. I feel light and remain happy. Because I never allow the problem to take control of me, I am able to master it.

Day 101

Value: Freedom

"The one whose mind is free is the one who can bring benefit to others."

Contemplation

We often feel that we do not have enough time for the "self". But the more we think only about ourselves, the less time we have for anyone else. Days pass by without us being able to bring any benefit to others, or to ourselves.

Application

Instead of thinking about myself all the time, I need to realize that helping others naturally helps me as well. To do this I first need to break free from the chains I have created in my own mind. Once I am free, I will be able to progress and bring benefit to all around me.

Day 102

Value: Patience

"Determination combined with patience brings success."

Contemplation

Sometimes we give up a task before we reach the end because we lack the patience to see things through. We then question why this has happened, and may even start to think of ourselves as a failure.

Application

Every time I begin a new task, I need to cultivate patience as well as determination. Patience helps me to wait for the fruit of my effort. If I am patient I am not in a hurry, and will not give up, even if it the result of my labor isn't immediately visible. Then I never experience failure, only a constant journey toward success.

DAY 103

VALUE: INTROSPECTION

"To pay attention to every act is to be a hero."

CONTEMPLATION

The role of the hero is something everyone is drawn to. Everyone wants to be in a position to get people's praise. When people praise us we feel good – when they don't we become disappointed. We are often dependent on people's appreciation to feel good about ourselves, and other people's views are not reliable.

APPLICATION

I become a hero when I pay attention to everything I do. I make sure that none of my words or actions are wasted or ordinary, and I strive for perfection in everything I do. When I pay attention in this way, I will be able to give my best at all times. I will feel satisfied, knowing that what I do is not as important as how well I do it.

DAY 104

VALUE: HAPPINESS

"Creativity comes when there is happiness."

CONTEMPLATION

When challenging situations head our way, there is a tendency to think in a cyclic way to try and overcome the problem. That is, the mind thinks of the same things again and again in the search for a solution. The longer this goes on, the more difficult it is to find a solution. There can be no happiness or peace of mind.

APPLICATION

Happiness touches the heart and enables creativity to emerge from within. When I am happy I am able to enjoy and make the best use of each moment. Someone who is happy doesn't wait for the right opportunity to be creative, but finds the creative potential in each moment. When I do something new, unique and different, I also have the satisfaction of having done my best.

Day 105

Value: Positivity

"As we think, so is our world."

Contemplation

In spite of our best efforts, if things don't turn out the way we expect them to, there is a tendency to get disheartened. The negative thoughts this brings about create further negative situations and we find that the quality of life does not improve.

Application

Instead of beginning to change situations that are going wrong, I need to work at the seed of these situations – my thoughts. I need to keep my thoughts positive in all circumstances. This will make my actions positive too, and slowly I will find things changing for the better.

DAY 106

VALUE: FAITH

"Where there is faith there is victory."

CONTEMPLATION

When we lack faith in ourselves we are assailed with doubts and questions about the self, others or situations. This doubt makes us lose our most important resource – our thoughts. We are not able to think well and make the right decisions. So victory eludes us and we further develop negative feelings.

APPLICATION

When I have faith, I see myself as lucky and thus receive co-operation from others. I am able to see and appreciate the simple things in life, which gives me the courage to go on. There is then no worry and I am untroubled by anything that changes around me. My thoughts then remain positive.

Day 107

Value: Sharing

"To have the spirit of sharing is to be constantly happy."

Contemplation

We often get caught up with our needs and desires. We become selfish, and focused on material possessions. The more we have, the more we want. We do not appreciate what we have, and become disappointed when our expectations are not fulfilled. We forget the pleasure that comes from sharing with others.

Application

I have so many resources that I can share with others. The more I become conscious of joy of giving, the more able I am to share both my material possessions and my inner resources. I will then discover new treasures within myself and be able to use them for the benefit of myself and others. This brings me constant satisfaction, as well as good wishes from others.

DAY 108

VALUE: LISTENING

"To listen to others frees us from repeating mistakes."

CONTEMPLATION

When other people criticize us, we often ignore them or focus on defending ourselves. We lose the power to listen, and are unable to accept the help that others are trying to give us. We fail to correct our mistakes and find that the same problems recur frequently.

APPLICATION

When people criticize things I say or do, I need to think about whether there is any truth in what they are saying. Although it might hurt to accept some of the things they tell me, I know they only want the best for me. Once I am aware of my weaknesses, I can change my behavior and constantly improve, moving toward success.

DAY 109

VALUE: HAPPINESS

"Understanding brings happiness."

CONTEMPLATION

Often we find ourselves caught up in situations which lead to negativity. Once we are aware of our negative feelings, we are unable to see things logically, which only leads to more negativity.

APPLICATION

To bring about positivity in my life, I need to try to understand why the situation has arisen. Then I will be able to remain happy under all circumstances. I will be free from the influence of others' negativity. Instead I will become a major source of positive influence to those around me.

DAY 110

VALUE: WISDOM

"The one who is wise is free from careless or negative talk about others."

CONTEMPLATION

When someone tells us something negative about another person, we tend to listen with great interest. This encourages the other person to continue talking about it. But such talk is not really useful for anyone and provides no solutions for the problem at hand.

APPLICATION

When someone is talking about another person's shortcomings, I need to question why I am listening: is this information of any use to me, or can I do anything about the situation? If not, I need to remind myself that there is no use in listening to such talk. Instead, I need to make an attempt to look at the positive qualities of the person in question, and think about how I can help everyone focus on these instead.

DAY 111

VALUE: HARMONY

"To understand others is to be in harmony with them."

CONTEMPLATION

We expect others to have similar attitudes and beliefs to ourselves. If another person's behavior or words are very different to what we are used to, we may find it hard to understand them. We may even develop a negative attitude toward them, and find we are not able to get along well.

APPLICATION

I need to recognize that like musical notes, we are all different. Only when I am able to harmonize with others can I create a beautiful tune. When I work with other people, I learn to understand them. In the process, I will also learn more about myself and how to use my strengths to support others.

Day 112

Value: Contentment

"To be content is to neither to get upset nor to upset others."

Contemplation

Sometimes we find that our words, actions or behavior upset others, even though this wasn't our intention. At the time it may be difficult to understand why others have become upset, and we may feel that they are being unreasonable.

Application

When others get upset with me, I need to reflect upon what I have done or said to try and work out why. I need to be aware of the effect I have on others and make an effort to change. This will bring about true contentment.

DAY 113

VALUE: INTROSPECTION

"The difficulty of the situation lies in one's own state of mind."

CONTEMPLATION

When we experience a difficult situation, we often become
overwhelmed by it. We become stuck, unable to think about
anything else. When this happens, the smallest problem can
easily turn into a bigger obstacle that becomes even more
difficult to overcome.

APPLICATION

The size of any problem depends on my state of mind. In
reality, it doesn't matter how small or large the problem is –
what matters is how I perceive it. When my mind is calm and
balanced, my confidence grows. If I believe I can overcome the
problem, I will do so.

Day 114

Value: Happiness

"Looking at things in a different light brings happiness."

Contemplation

When everything is the same, we become bored and unhappy. If we continue to think and act in the same way, we become stuck in a rut. We are unable to become excited about new situations and opportunities. This drains our positive energy, leaving us lifeless and unenthusiastic

Application

I find happiness when I try new ways of dealing with life's situations. The potential and the energy of my mind are channeled in a positive way then and I feel fulfillment and satisfaction. Life itself becomes more beautiful.

DAY 115

VALUE: DISCERNMENT

"The one who discerns well can bring about real benefit."

CONTEMPLATION

Everyone naturally works for their own benefit and that of others. But sometimes others do not seem to appreciate our contribution. This is usually because we haven't been able to recognize what they need. We tend to give what we feel is important, but this may mean ignoring someone else's needs.

APPLICATION

Someone who discerns well is able to understand other people's needs and give accordingly. Whatever that person does helps others. When I am able to help the right person at the right time, I am able to win their trust. I should expect nothing in return, but the satisfaction of helping at the right time.

Day 116

Value: Self-Growth

"To develop our gifts is to enrich our lives."

Contemplation

When we interact with others, often we are overly concerned with their negative aspects. Their gifts become hidden. The more we emphasize negativity, the more difficult it is to see past it. We fill ourselves and others with negativity, often without even realizing it.

Application

Becoming aware of our own gifts and those of others fills life with beauty. When I am aware of others' unique gifts, I can encourage them to develop them. Using my own gifts enriches others as well as myself. At times of need, I am able to draw on these qualities.

DAY 117

VALUE: SELF-RESPECT

"Every reaction is a reflection of one's own self-respect."

CONTEMPLATION

If we have low self-respect, even the smallest situation brings forth a strong negative reaction. We continue to blame circumstances and use them as excuses not to take responsibility for ourselves. We feel helpless and unable to do anything about situations. This reaction to difficult situations only makes matters worse.

APPLICATION

When my self-respect is high, I am able to remain positive even in the most negative situations. This allows me to control the situation, rather than letting it control me.

DAY 118

VALUE: COMMUNICATION

"Words are effective when they are spoken with good wishes."

CONTEMPLATION

Although we speak with a great deal of logic so that other people understand our meaning, sometimes our words are misunderstood and misinterpreted. Many conflicts arise because of this, spoiling our relationships.

APPLICATION

What I say is important – but much more important is how I say it and with what feeling. I need to keep myself free from any kind of attitude when I communicate with people. This happens naturally when I have good wishes for others – them my words become truly effective.

DAY 119

VALUE: SWEETNESS

"To speak from the heart means to spread sweetness around."

CONTEMPLATION

When speaking to others we usually speak from our head, or intellect. Words spoken from the head rarely touch the hearts of others. This means they don't create any impact and are soon forgotten.

APPLICATION

The solution lies in touching the hearts of others when I speak. To do that, I need to speak with my heart as well as my head and fill my words with love. When I communicate with others in this way my words spread sweetness around.

DAY 120

VALUE: FLEXIBILITY

"To be free from weakness means having the power to change."

CONTEMPLATION

We all have weaknesses that make it difficult for us to adapt to the needs of a situation. Our weaknesses can make us inflexible and blind to new possibilities. Then we find it difficult to work with our weaknesses, which breeds negativity.

APPLICATION

To have the ability to adapt gives me the ability to handle any situation. I become as flexible and beautiful as pure gold, which transforms when heated into something beautiful. I embrace change, and this equips me to enjoy the beauty I create and the joy I spread.

DAY 121

VALUE: HAPPINESS

"To find reasons to be happy is to increase happiness."

CONTEMPLATION

Sometimes we find ourselves caught up with feelings of negativity from which we are not able to free ourselves. At such a time even situations with no great significance are seen in a negative light as the mind searches for reasons to be sad and sorrowful. We seek sympathy and reassurance from others in an effort to make ourselves feel better. But this only works for a short time.

APPLICATION

When I am happy, I start seeing everything in a positive light. It is as though I am wearing colored glasses: the whole world takes on a brighter hue. I no longer see negativity in everything around me; everything I see and experience only increases my happiness.

Day 122

Value: Positivity

"To have positive thoughts is to be a well-wisher."

Contemplation

We usually want the best for everyone and ensure that everything goes well. But we really don't know much about service. Our idea of service is limited to the physical act of helping another person. But thoughts are often more powerful, because our thoughts affect everything we do and say.

Application

To be full of good thoughts is to be a true well-wisher. When I am filled with the treasure of knowledge I am able to spread positive vibrations through my mind. I have good wishes for everyone I meet, and all my words and actions bring benefit to others.

DAY 123

VALUE: CO-OPERATION

"The best way to get co-operation is to give co-operation."

CONTEMPLATION

Usually when we want help, we look for it from those closest to us. We expect them to understand what we need and then to give us what we need. We constantly look for support and help – this doesn't allow us to fully explore our talents and use them for everyone's benefit.

APPLICATION

The best way to co-operate is to use the energy of the mind to create good wishes and pure feelings toward others and for the success of a task. When I co-operate with others in this way, I will receive their co-operation when I need it most.

DAY 124

VALUE: GIVING

"To understand the spirit of giving is to be constantly happy."

CONTEMPLATION

We often expect others to give to us, rather than the other way around. When we constantly expect to receive help from others, we lose sight of our own resources. And if others do not fulfill our expectations, we tend to feel low and dissatisfied with life, and we may blame others.

APPLICATION

Instead of waiting for others to give to me, I need to think about what I can do for others. Today I will think about being less dependent on other people and contemplate the talents that lie within me. The more I am able to give to others, the more I will grow.

DAY 125

VALUE: LOVE

"To have true love means creating an environment where others can grow."

CONTEMPLATION

In relationships, we often expect things from those we get close to. These expectations can stifle the other person and also stop us from allowing the other person to develop in a way that is right for them.

APPLICATION

I express true love when I create the right environment for those I love. This is an environment in which they can grow. And in order to do this I must stop expecting those I am closest to behave according to my agenda. I need to support them in their personal growth, wherever that might take them.

DAY 126

VALUE: DETERMINATION

"To work with determination ensures success."

CONTEMPLATION

When difficult situations come our way, we are not always confident of our success. So although there is a chance to do something, we are not able to give our best. Each new situation is perceived as a threat. Once fear creeps in, the situation worsens, until all chances of success disappear.

APPLICATION

When I am determined I am confident of success. This confidence allows me to do everything necessary to succeed. I never let go of anything halfway, but see to it that the task is completed. With every obstacle my determination increases so that I progress at every step.

Day 127

Value: Flexibility

"To be flexible is to enjoy everything that life brings."

Contemplation

When we plan for the day ahead, we sometimes find that we are not able to do everything we had hoped. Things come up unexpectedly. When this happens, we are not able to be happy and find it difficult to do what we need, or to work at our best.

Application

It is as important to be flexible in my thoughts as it is to be particular about my daily schedule. Flexibility allows me to accommodate unforeseen situations and helps me make best use of my time, resources and opportunities. When I am flexible I enjoy everything that life brings.

DAY 128

VALUE: GIVING

"To have commitment for self-progress is to be a giver."

CONTEMPLATION

Although we have much, we are always looking for more. We have great expectations of people and situations and constantly think about what we can gain from them. Such expectations make us dependent on others for self-progress. If we do this, we only experience progress when things are going right or when others are co-operative.

APPLICATION

Instead of thinking about what I want to get, I need to pay more attention to what I have, so that I can do my best using these resources to acquire what I want. Doing this allows me to enjoy constant progress, whether the situations I encounter are positive or not.

DAY 129

VALUE: INTROSPECTION

"To understand the true cause of one's own weakness is to gain the power to overcome it."

CONTEMPLATION

When we recognize a weakness within we often make an effort to overcome it. But sometimes, despite our best efforts, the same weakness keeps returning. This is because we have not got to the root of the problem and removed it.

APPLICATION

Before I try to remove a weakness working within me, I need to understand the cause of that weakness. To do this I need to reflect on why that weakness is present and what is lacking within me. Once I find the cause I need to make an effort to fill myself with the corresponding virtue, which will drive the weakness out for good.

Day 130

Value: Positivity

"A single positive thought can make the mind powerful."

Contemplation

When a negative thought comes to mind regarding ourselves, another person or a situation, more negative thoughts follow – about things that went wrong in the past, for instance – and we find ourselves overwhelmed by negativity.

Application

I need to take the challenge of thinking positively even in the most negative situation. This will help me break the cycle of negativity. The positive thoughts need not be connected to the present situation; I just need to conjure up any thought that will guide me toward a more life-affirming way of thinking.

DAY 131

VALUE: TOLERANCE

"The one who understands the power of truth is tolerant."

CONTEMPLATION

When someone disbelieves us, we usually argue back and try to prove our point. Yet we find that the more we talk, the less people listen. Unable to convince them, we end up frustrated.

APPLICATION

When someone challenges the truth of my words, I should think about whether they might be right. Rather than stubbornly clinging to my point of view, I should embrace this as an opportunity to learn. Even if I am correct in my thinking, if I become able to understand someone else's point of view without getting angry or refusing to listen, I become tolerant.

DAY 132

VALUE: KNOWLEDGE

"To bring knowledge into practice is to ensure success."

CONTEMPLATION

Often theory and practice are two separate things. We have a great deal of knowledge, but do not apply it in a practical way. We might talk about how we could do something, for instance, but never actually get around to doing it. We waste time thinking about things rather than actually doing them.

APPLICATION

I need to make the effort to start applying knowledge in a practical way. The first step is to understand what I need to do. Then I need to sustain my thoughts by turning them into action. Then not only will my life will be enriched, all my thoughts will have power.

DAY 133

VALUE: DETERMINATION

"Determined thoughts disperse the clouds of negative situations."

CONTEMPLATION

A lot of negative situations are bound to come our way, resulting in grief, pain and disappointment. At the time, such difficulties feels insurmountable and seem to last forever.

APPLICATION

I need to recognize that the difficulties I face are like passing clouds. These clouds gather around me at times, but are only temporary – sooner or later they will fade away. Understanding that no problem lasts forever will help me develop the determination I need to work on my problems. I will then be able to face any situation with ease.

Day 134

VALUE: NON-VIOLENCE

"True non-violence is not to hurt others even through words."

CONTEMPLATION

Most people could not imagine hurting anyone physically. But sometimes we hurt others through our words. This creates negativity in others which in turn affects us negatively. Hurtful words affect everyone profoundly.

APPLICATION

In order to live a life that is truly non-violent, I must pay special attention to my words. Words that don't hurt others are the result of positive thoughts based on good wishes and benevolent feelings for others.

Day 135

Value: Focus

"The right awareness brings power."

Contemplation

We are often aware of what we need to do to make life better or more meaningful, but find ourselves unable to bring that understanding into practice. Because it is difficult, we may give up after trying several times without success.

Application

The practice of a powerful thought such as "victory is my birthright" or "I am the master of my life" helps me become aware of my own power. If I focus on potent thoughts like this today and every day, my confidence will grow and I will develop the power to act in the way I desire.

DAY 136

VALUE: GIVING

"Generosity brings success."

CONTEMPLATION

All of us have a many gifts – skills, talents, or knowledge – which we don't use as much as we could. Just like our muscles, when we don't use them for a long time, they begin to waste away. So when we need those gifts, we might find they are no longer there for us to call on.

APPLICATION

The more generously I use my gifts to benefit others, the more they will be available for me at the right time. When I am generous with my gifts I will find myself moving easily forward with the blessings I receive in return.

DAY 137

VALUE: BALANCE

"Success comes to the one who maintains balance, being
equally master and child."

CONTEMPLATION

We rarely offer advice unless we are confident that we know
what we are talking about. But when we do make a suggestion,
we expect people to act upon it. If they decide not to, we often
take it as a criticism, or the implication that they don't trust us.

APPLICATION

I need to maintain a perfect balance between being a master
and a child. As a master, I am able to offer others advice. But I
need to maintain the consciousness of a child while listening to
advice myself. That means being ready to accept comments or
criticism without feeling hurt.

DAY 138

VALUE: INTROSPECTION

"Silence enables one to listen to the solution to difficult situations."

CONTEMPLATION

In challenging situations, we tend to think a lot to try to find the right solution. But often the more we think, the further we move away from the solution as the mind travels round in circles.

APPLICATION

Inner silence means creating a state of inner calm. By listening to my inner self, I am able to break free from problems and discover solutions. I will be confident of doing the right thing, and able to use the best of my talent, creativity and inner power to do whatever has to be done.

DAY 139

VALUE: PEACE

"The more I experience peace within myself, the more
positivity I will have in my life."

CONTEMPLATION

Usually we try to address our weaknesses by working on each
one separately. We might be able to overcome some of them,
but as they are all connected to our other weaknesses, we soon
find the same problems re-emerging. Negativity then
overwhelms us, influencing all our thoughts, words and
actions.

APPLICATION

I first need to make a promise to myself to maintain my inner
positivity. I then need to practise keeping my mind calm. This
calmness will bring contentment, leading to increasing feelings
of positivity. The more I strengthen my inner positivity, the
better able I will be to vanquish my weaknesses.

Day 140

Value: Freedom

"Freedom starts in the mind, not by cutting ropes."

Contemplation

We often feel as though we are tied down by situations or people. This makes us feel uncomfortable, and we try to break free. But we soon find it is not easy to do so – and understand that the chains we are trying to break are actually a product of our own minds.

Application

I need to understand that the chains holding me back are within my mind. I also need to realize that whatever happens to me is my own choice – nothing is forced on me. When I take responsibility for myself in this way I will learn not to complain, but to make the best of every situation. Only then can I become truly free.

DAY 141

VALUE: INNER STRENGTH

"Difficulties and challenges bring out our hidden treasures."

CONTEMPLATION

When we are faced with challenges, we sometimes feel that we
are not strong enough, or that we won't be good enough.
Instead of looking at a challenging situation as an opportunity
to develop and progress, we experience a lot of negativity.

APPLICATION

When I have confidence in myself and learn how to use the
treasures that are hidden within me, I will be able to remain
strong in the most troublesome situations. Then difficulties will
be transformed – with my newfound inner strength they will
appear instead as welcome opportunities to grow even stronger.

DAY 142

VALUE: PATIENCE

"Where there is peace there is patience."

CONTEMPLATION

We are often impulsive or react hastily without giving ourselves time to think or understand a situation properly. Because of this lack of patience, we lose out on many things, often without even realizing.

APPLICATION

I need to make a conscious effort to keep my mind peaceful, particularly when I encounter difficulties. Such a state of mind nurtures patience: peace generates power, which in turn brings patience.

DAY 143

VALUE: UNDERSTANDING

"To understand is to be open to learning."

CONTEMPLATION

When someone says something we don't like, we usually find fault with those people themselves. This is a result of not understanding the true nature of the situation.

APPLICATION

I need to understand that people have appeared in my life for a reason and that I can learn from everything that happens through my interactions with them. Recognizing this fact will stop me from blaming others and start me on the road to personal growth.

DAY 144

VALUE: DETERMINATION

"Determination breaks the barriers that difficulties create."

CONTEMPLATION

We cannot avoid barriers that block our way and seem to stop us progressing in life. When we lack determination, we become stuck behind these barriers, and find ourselves losing interest in life and all its opportunities.

APPLICATION

Whenever barriers appear, I need to remind myself that I can use them as a way to challenge myself to move forward. When I remind myself of this, I get in touch with the determination I need to work to overcome those barriers.

Day 145

Value: Humility

"The power of humility cools the fire of anger."

Contemplation

When we react to anger with anger, we inflame an already hostile situation and let ourselves down, too – because we have within us the power to pour water on the flames.

Application

Today if my words or deeds are met with an angry word or gesture, I will not react in the same manner. I will cultivate patience and feel humble rather than self-righteous. This is the way to diffuse angry feelings and allow my more powerful self to emerge.

DAY 146

VALUE: SELF-CONTROL

"True victory is inner stability."

CONTEMPLATION

Whenever things are going well and success follows it's easy to feel on top of our affairs and in a stable state of mind. But it only takes one challenge to topple this stable tower, which can be undercut by fear and anxiety.

APPLICATION

I need to change the way I respond to negative situations – today I will remind myself that although decisions may be out of my hands, I have a choice about how I choose to respond to them. Once I realize this, I regain control over the situation and my state of mind returns to stability.

Day 147

Value: Hope

"To have hope in the face of negativity brings about real change."

Contemplation

When we see someone behaving very negatively, we tend to write them off, thinking – and saying to others – that this person is hopeless and can never change. This prevents that person from being able to change for the better.

Application

Hope holds the key to transforming someone from a negative into a positive state. When I meet someone who has fallen into the trap of negativity, I need to make special effort to offer them a supportive environment in which they can develop their potential. By showing them how much I believe in them, I help them bring about a positive change.

Day 148

Value: Positivity

"Those who have the power to transform negativity into positivity are constantly cheerful."

Contemplation

The usual reaction to negativity is to feel disheartened and to lose our inner contentment. Once we become aware of someone's negative attitude toward us, it becomes difficult, even if we try, to forgive them and forget the harm done.

Application

The more I am able to see people as uniquely talented individuals, the sooner I will be able to forgive them their weaknesses – this is a sure way to become constantly cheerful.

DAY 149

VALUE: BALANCE

"The balance between firmness and love brings change in others."

CONTEMPLATION

When we want to bring about change in others, we need to speak firmly. But sometimes this firmness takes on the form of rudeness because we don't combine it with the right attitude.

APPLICATION

When I want to help someone change, I need to be firm as well as loving. Being balanced in this way makes my words and actions have a greater effect on the other person, and then I will be easily able to bring about the desired result.

DAY 150

VALUE: CONTENTMENT

"True contentment brings as much contentment to others as to the self."

CONTEMPLATION

When we have to do something, we usually do it the way we prefer. We often don't think about how others might feel. Instead, we focus on our own happiness, ignoring how the act affects others.

APPLICATION

I need to make sure my actions do not make anyone feel uncomfortable or upset. I need to reflect on the things I do and how they affect others, then make changes to the way I habitually act. When I consider others before myself, my actions bring contentment to myself and others.

Day 151

Value: Self-control

"To be a master is to be free from one's own weaknesses."

Contemplation

We are often under the control of our own weaknesses, especially in difficult situations, which tend to bring out the worst in us. When our weaknesses do get the better of us, we are more likely to give up than persevere in the face of opposition.

Application

I need to develop the consciousness that I am a master: the weakness within me is my own creation, and so it is totally in my control. When I develop this consciousness I will be to overcome my weaknesses easily, instead of feeling bound by them.

DAY 152

VALUE: CO-OPERATION

"True co-operation brings easy success in every task."

CONTEMPLATION

To be co-operative to someone who is being good to you, and to get the co-operation of "good" people is easy. But other people's co-operation does not come consistently. When we lack co-operation, it affects the task and our state of mind negatively.

APPLICATION

True co-operation is a result of the vision of hope and faith I have in every individual I come in contact with. When I have this vision, I am better able to co-operate in the right way. And I am more likely to gain their co-operation at all times and for all tasks – because I will be inspiring the best in them.

DAY 153

VALUE: HAPPINESS

"True happiness is an experience which touches others."

CONTEMPLATION

Even in positive situations, we sometimes seem lacking in happiness ourselves or find that we are unable to make others happy, but cannot understand why.

APPLICATION

When I am really happy, I have a natural desire to share it with others. This urge to share helps me to spread my happiness. If the happiness is based on truth, no harm will follow for myself or others, and all concerned will benefit from my state of mind.

DAY 154

VALUE: DETERMINATION

"To say 'I will do it' ensures success."

CONTEMPLATION

When something difficult comes our way, the first thought is often, "It is difficult, but I will try to do it." But saying "I will try" brings doubt into the mind. When doubt creeps in, we often overlook things that help us become successful.

APPLICATION

Saying "I will do it" is the key to success. This thought is filled with power, which in turn helps me make every effort to bring about that success. I will naturally do my best, using everything available to me. When I am determined to succeed, I find that other people and situations work in my favour to help me achieve my goal.

DAY 155

VALUE: LOVE

"Love makes things easy."

CONTEMPLATION

When something difficult has to be done, we sometimes feel bad about the task. If we see it in a negative light, we can no longer love it. The task seems even more difficult, and this makes it hard to make the effort we need to help us succeed.

APPLICATION

When I approach things with love, I find ways and means to accomplish what I set out to do. No task seems heavy or difficult. Love also draws good wishes and help from those around me. Then every task becomes easy to accomplish.

DAY 156

VALUE: INTROSPECTION

"To be connected to the inner self is to be positive."

CONTEMPLATION

When we face negative situations, we either become negative or try to move away from the situation. But that's only a temporary solution: the negative thoughts, feelings and emotions will continue to follow us.

APPLICATION

By connecting to my inner self, I can stay positive even in negative circumstances. Deep within me are the most beautiful qualities of peace, love and happiness, which I mistakenly look for outside. Developing these qualities helps me to stay positive regardless of the circumstances.

DAY 157

VALUE: SELFLESSNESS

"True service is always free from expectation."

CONTEMPLATION

It's natural to help others when we see
them in need. We don't expect anything from them in return at
the time. When we need help or support ourselves, we expect
to receive it from those we helped. If they don't give us this
help in return, we may feel hurt or disappointment.

APPLICATION

When I help others, I need to remind myself not to expect
anything from them in return. Whatever help I have given will
come back to me at the right time. The seed I have sown will
not be wasted but will bear fruit when the time is right.

DAY 158

VALUE: HONESTY

"To be honest means to experience progress."

CONTEMPLATION

We usually understand honesty to mean freedom from lies or falsehood. But although we try to be honest in this way, it is not always possible because of the situations we find ourselves in.

APPLICATION

True honesty is more connected with my innate nature than just being free from lies. When I am honest I will see what I need to do in every situation. I am able to bring about a change in such a way that I never repeat the mistake I have made.

DAY 159

VALUE: GIVING

"True servers are those who are content."

CONTEMPLATION

Sometimes we try to fill a gap in our lives by doing something good or by serving others. But we may be motivated by the contentment service brings, rather than the opportunity to help others.

APPLICATION

Before I can serve others, I must be content within myself. Only when I am content can I serve selflessly in whatever way necessary. When I am content I am free from expectation and able to use all my resources for others' benefit.

Day 160

Value: Self-control

"To be a master means using the powers I have at the
right time."

Contemplation

Each of us has several powers, which we can use to help us in
various situations. But we are not always able to use the right
the right power at the right time. Despite having the power
within, we are unable to use it when required.

Application

I need to practise mastering all my inner powers. The more I
practise, the more I will find my powers working in the way I
need them to. When I have complete self-control I will be able
to use the right power at the right time to ensure success.

DAY 161

VALUE: INNER STRENGTH

"Inner strength comes from facing problems rather than avoiding them."

CONTEMPLATION

When we encounter problems we tend to blame people or situations. We feel that these problems have come to take away our power. We wish something will happen to change the situation so that we can be free of the problem. But it seems to take a long time before the situation changes.

APPLICATION

The only way I can be free from a problem is to create a solution. I need to realize that the situation will not change on its own. Drawing on my inner strength helps me find a solution to the problem. I then discover that I am capable of far more than I realized.

DAY 162

VALUE: SELF-RESPECT

"The one who has self-respect is free from aggression."

CONTEMPLATION

In difficult situations, we can feel helpless. This creates tension, which often gets expressed in the form of aggression. This kind of aggression cannot be suppressed or controlled and so simple things become difficult and relationships fill with conflict.

APPLICATION

When I respect myself, I can keep my mind calm. I do not react to situations in a negative way. Instead, I take time to understand the situation and respond in the right way. I make decisions in a composed state of mind, and so I find myself relaxed even in the most difficult circumstance.

DAY 163

VALUE: POSITIVITY

"To understand the treasure of thoughts makes them powerful."

CONTEMPLATION

We pay special attention to make sure our actions reflect our best self. We also think about the words we use. But we hardly ever focus on our thoughts. When certain thoughts become repetitive they gain a hold over us.

APPLICATION

It is important for me to get into the habit of having positive thoughts. When my thoughts are positive, they become powerful. Each thought becomes a treasure from which I can draw power. My words and actions naturally become more powerful too.

DAY 164

VALUE: CO-OPERATION

"Good wishes win co-operation."

CONTEMPLATION

Using force or anger as a means to get things done is common. But it doesn't inspire good feeling in others. Although the task gets completed, it is neither done as well as it could be, nor do we get real satisfaction from it.

APPLICATION

It is more important for me to focus on having positive feelings and good wishes for those around me than on getting a task done. If I look for the good in people, I cannot help but love them. When I express that love, I create a positive environment in which all work together toward a shared goal. I no longer have to worry about getting others to co-operate with me. Instead, it happens naturally.

DAY 165

VALUE: INTROSPECTION

"To understand the significance of everything that happens is
to be light."

CONTEMPLATION

When something happens that contradicts what we expect, we
find it difficult to understand. We tend to get upset or
disturbed, which further confuses the mind, leaving us
confounded and unable to do anything to correct the situation.

APPLICATION

Everything happens for a reason. When things don't happen the
way I expect them to, I need to try hard to work out why. If I
understand the reason behind an event, I will no longer feel
weighed down by worries and confusion. I will become light
and free.

DAY 166

VALUE: COMMUNICATION

"To be economical with words gets things done more easily."

CONTEMPLATION

We expend a lot of time and energy in trying to express ourselves. When we say too much, most of what we say is wasted. People switch off and stop listening.

APPLICATION

A lot can be said in a few words. When I think carefully about what I need to communicate, I realize I can do it more easily with fewer words. This saves my time and energy, and that of others. Other people then become more willing to listen to me, and understand what I need them to do.

DAY 167

VALUE: GIVING

"To be a giver is to experience constant happiness."

CONTEMPLATION

Sometimes we find ourselves in situations in which we try to make others happy, even though in doing so we neglect ourselves and experience sorrow. We often do things for the sake of others, even though it is difficult. And if this gift is not recognized or appreciated, we tend to get upset.

APPLICATION

I will experience the greatest happiness if I give without expecting anything in return. I have to learn to give wisely. When I give with a pure heart, I will experience happiness and make those around me happy too.

DAY 168

VALUE: LEARNING FROM MISTAKES

"To learn brings about a practical change."

CONTEMPLATION

We can learn a great deal from everything we do – the people
we meet and the situations we find ourselves in. But we often
make the same mistakes again and again. Although we may
have understood the problem, we are unable to bring about
real change.

APPLICATION

When I think I have learnt from a mistake, I need to question
whether I have really understood it, or if there is still more that
I can learn. This will help me make sure I don't repeat the same
mistake and this is the key to real change.

DAY 169

VALUE: WISDOM

"To be wise is to be prepared for the tests of life."

CONTEMPLATION

We usually prepare for the tests of life only after we are faced with them. Although we try hard, without being well-prepared, it is hard to progress. To anticipate what might happen and be well-prepared beforehand is to use our inner resources well.

APPLICATION

In order to move forward constantly, I need to be prepared well in advance. I can only do this when I reflect on and learn from all the experiences of the past. With this inner preparation I can face all life's tests. I have all the skills I need to deal with the present.

Day 170

Value: Co-operation

"When everyone one is working toward a common task,
co-operation becomes easy."

Contemplation

To win other people's co-operation, we need to share both the task and the information regarding the task with everyone involved. If we communicate our motives using easy and simple language, everyone will understand. This helps create team spirit, when everyone naturally does their best for the good of all involved.

Application

Whenever I take up a new task that involves working with several people, I need to let everyone know everything before we get started. Even the small details can make a big difference to other's understanding and help them prioritize tasks. When everyone works together in harmony, we are able to complete the task quickly and efficiently.

Day 171

Value: Tolerance

"True tolerance is free from negative feelings."

Contemplation

Tolerance means accepting that which we find difficult. When we have to tolerate something, we feel that we have a lot to endure. With effort, we adapt to the situation, even though we may harbour negative feelings. This is not real tolerance.

Application

Tolerance is the ability to use my inner power to deal with a difficult situation in the right way. When I work on improving myself with each challenge, I equip myself to move forward. I free myself from negative feelings, and experience progress at every step.

DAY 172

VALUE: INNER STRENGTH

"The more I overcome my weaknesses, the more benefit there is
for myself and others."

CONTEMPLATION

The normal reaction to situations that hold a threat for us is to
react with our weaknesses. There's a problem with such a
reaction: each time we draw on our weaknesses, they become
stronger, and become ingrained in our nature.

APPLICATION

I need to remind myself that only when I free myself from my
weaknesses can I bring benefit to myself or to others. This
thought will enable me to put in constant effort to overcome
my flaws.

DAY 173

VALUE: RESPONSIBILITY

"True responsibility brings inner lightness and joy."

CONTEMPLATION

When we are responsible for something or someone, it can become a burden. When responsibility weighs heavily on us, we feel trapped, like a caged bird. We long to escape and spread our wings. When we feel this way, we do not fulfill our responsibilities as well as we are able.

APPLICATION

The true meaning of responsibility is not just taking care of duties; it has more to do with engaging with the task and doing everything with a sense of purpose. When I think about my responsibilities with this attitude I find things getting easier and I receive help at every step. I am able to accomplish more work with a light heart and I enjoy everything I do.

DAY 174

VALUE: BEING PRESENT

"To be in the present is to make the best use of it."

CONTEMPLATION

When we become dissatisfied with life, there is a tendency to look back and reminisce about times gone by. We sometimes wish we could return to a particular moment in time. Or we wonder what could have happened if we had made a different decision. Soon we become trapped in thoughts and memories, and fail to make the most of the present.

APPLICATION

I have to realize that the only time I have any control over is now, and I have the power to make each moment count. The way I choose to use my time now will also have an effect on my future. The only way I can make a beautiful future for myself is by making the best of the present moment.

Day 175

Value: Self-control

"Self-control means having the ability to channel thoughts in the right direction."

Contemplation

Normally we think of self-control as trying to force the mind not to think in a particular way. It is perceived as something to do with suppressing emotion. Of course, we find that we are unable to do so. This usually means we give up altogether and consider self-control difficult.

Application

Self-control means mastering my thoughts, feelings and emotions. However big the challenges may be, I am able to channel my thoughts in the right direction. I never let my thoughts wander, so I never have to worry about regaining control. This makes my mind creative so that I find the solutions to problems more easily.

DAY 176

VALUE: CO-OPERATION

"The best way to teach is by example."

CONTEMPLATION

When we are trying to help someone learn, we use many words trying to explain a point. We want to convince the other person of what we are saying and expect them to behave according to our desire. Yet it is not so easy to convince others, and people continue to behave according to what they feel is right.

APPLICATION

Actions are more convincing than words. When people see me doing something, it creates a greater impact than if I had just explained it to them. My actions become a source of inspiration that brings about a change in others.

DAY 177

VALUE: COMMUNICATION

"The art of listening enables me to support those around me."

CONTEMPLATION

When I hear something negative about someone, I am often influenced by it, even if I have only had positive experiences with the person in question. This brings about a change in my attitude and behavior toward that person.

APPLICATION

I need to learn the art of listening to enable me to respond in the right way. When someone describes another person in a negative light I need to understand what that person was thinking and feeling at the time. When I do this I will be able to support him without prejudice.

DAY 178

VALUE: CALMNESS

"True victory lies in keeping the mind peaceful in chaotic conditions."

CONTEMPLATION

It is easy to have pessimistic feelings and react in a negative way when there is chaos all around. We usually find several reasons to justify such behavior. But we do not feel positive or happy about our reaction, and there is no victory in expressing negative feelings, nor in suppressing them.

APPLICATION

To attain peace when something goes wrong, I need to keep my mind open to the advantages hidden in the situation. Then I can accept and learn. This will create positive feelings, which will help me find the solution to a problem. I will transform every defeat into a victory.

DAY 179

VALUE: DETERMINATION

"Determination breaks the barriers that difficulties create."

CONTEMPLATION

Difficulties are a part of life: we cannot avoid them. When they arise, they often create barriers which prevent us from moving forward. We become stuck and frustrated at our inability to move forward.

APPLICATION

Whenever difficult situations come my way, I need to remind myself to look at them not as barriers, but as stepping stones to progress. Although it may still take a great deal of effort to leap from one to the next, my determination to succeed will give me the strength I need.

DAY 180

VALUE: RESPONSIBILITY

"To take responsibility for one's actions allows the self to grow."

CONTEMPLATION

It is easy to blame others or the situation for difficulties. But if we look for excuses all the time, we are not able to do anything to support our personal growth. Life becomes a constant struggle and we begin to feel bound in by situations.

APPLICATION

When I am conscious of my own growth I am aware of my thoughts, feelings and emotions, and I understand how they influence my behavior. I then become able to take responsibility for my own choices and actions. I am no longer bound by any situation and begin to feel free.

DAY 181

VALUE: CO-OPERATION

"True progress lies in the power of co-operation."

CONTEMPLATION

In today's world, we often think of competition as a way to progress. Comparing ourselves with others can inspire us to perform better. Sometimes, we avoid helping others because it might hinder our own progress. But what we often overlook is that we cannot do everything on our own. We need to learn to work with others if we want to experience true success.

APPLICATION

True co-operation is the ability to help others and to allow them to help us. I need to learn that other people have a lot to teach me, and that I have something to offer them. When I learn to co-operate with people, we all make more progress.

DAY 182

VALUE: FOCUS

"To be focused is to be constantly successful."

CONTEMPLATION

Many of us have a tendency to postpone even the most important things to the last moment. We assume we will be able to get things done later. But sometimes the unexpected intervenes and everything collapses under the added strain.

APPLICATION

When I remain focused I am able to prioritize. I understand that small tasks can be as important as the larger ones, and I make sure I get them done at the right time. I make sure I leave time for the unexpected, too. This lifts the pressure and allows me to give my best in every situation.

DAY 183

VALUE: HAPPINESS

"Long-lasting happiness emerges from working constantly toward a specific goal."

CONTEMPLATION

We tend look for happiness in all we do. If we cannot see the results of effort, we are not inspired to complete the task. This attitude means that although we might experience happiness for a short time, it will never be long lasting.

APPLICATION

Real, long-lasting happiness comes from committing myself to a specific goal. When I am focused on what I want to achieve, the little things that I find difficult or which don't give me immediate happiness don't get in my way. I move toward my goal with happiness.

DAY 184

VALUE: CALMNESS

"Calmness of the mind brings accuracy in judgment."

CONTEMPLATION

Whenever a challenge requires us to make an accurate judgment, we tend to panic and start to worry about whether we will make the right choice. Whatever decisions we take with such a state of mind tend to go wrong.

APPLICATION

In challenging situations, I need to make sure my mind is calm before I make any decisions. To be able to do this, I need to practise calming my mind on a regular basis. Once I have mastered the technique, I will be able to make decisions much more easily, even in difficult situations.

Day 185

Value: Forgiveness

"To forgive the self is to have the ability to forgive others too."

Contemplation

When someone makes a mistake it can be difficult to forgive them. We have a tendency to remind ourselves of that mistake again and again. Though we might try hard to understand what caused them to make the mistake, we often find it difficult. If we cannot understand the other person's behavior, we find it difficult to forgive them.

Application

When I love myself and am able to learn from all that happens, I am able to forgive myself, too. I can use what I have learned to progress. I become able to understand the other person's perspective and I am able to forgive them.

DAY 186

VALUE: INTROSPECTION

"To exercise the mind regularly keeps it healthy."

CONTEMPLATION

Whenever we have negative thoughts, we try to stop them. We know they are not good for us and they drain us of energy, so we try to avoid them or change them. Because we are not always able to succeed in doing so, we begin to accept these kinds of thoughts as part of our lives.

APPLICATION

I need to get into the habit of exercising my mind in order to keep it healthy. To exercise the mind means creating and stabilizing whatever consciousness is required at that time. That means if I need peace, I can to hold that thought for however long I want to. This prepares me to deal with difficult times.

DAY 187

VALUE: KNOWLEDGE

"True knowledge gives us the power to perform the right action at the right time."

CONTEMPLATION

We usually enjoy learning new things, but it is often more difficult to translate our knowledge into practice.

APPLICATION

When I hear or see things that I think would help me, I must make the effort to incorporate them into my life. When I do this consistently, I recognize the power of knowledge to transform what I do. The more I use my knowledge in a practical way, the more I am able to tap into the power within me. As I continue to apply each point of knowledge to the right situation in my life, I equip myself with the skills necessary to deal with any situation.

DAY 188

VALUE: GIVING

"What we give is what we get."

CONTEMPLATION

Usually we wait for others to be good to us, so that we can respond in the same way. But people do not always behave in a positive way. Despite our best intentions, we are not always consistent with the way we treat others, either, and this often leads to confusion and hurt feelings.

APPLICATION

I need to understand that whatever I give will be reflected back to me. If I project peace and happiness toward those around me, I will get it back. But this should neither be superficial (at the level of words and actions only) nor inconsistent. When I am able to give without expecting anything in return, what I give will return to me quite naturally.

DAY 189

VALUE: CO-OPERATION

"Even the most difficult task is made easy with the co-operation of all."

CONTEMPLATION

When given a responsibility we usually plan to do it alone. It just seems simpler not to involve too many people. It also helps us to avoid the different kinds of personalities that we may find tricky to deal with. This attitude deprives us of others' support and co-operation.

APPLICATION

When involved in a big task, I need to see to it that I involve as many people as necessary. When I involve lots of people I gain access to all their specialties – and there's sure to be someone there with the skills to make even the most difficult task easy.

DAY 190

VALUE: WISDOM

"To be wise is to see the order in everything that is happening."

CONTEMPLATION

When difficult situations arise, we often find it hard to understand why the situation has occurred at that time. Without understanding this, we are unable to respond to the situation in the right way, which means we experience failure again and again.

APPLICATION

Wisdom teaches me that everything that happens in life is significant. Nothing is the fruit of chance, but is due to what I did yesterday. This means that whatever I do today will have an impact on what happens tomorrow. I will think about this today and initiate wise acts.

DAY 191

VALUE: CONTENTMENT

"The one with contentment neither becomes upset nor upsets others."

CONTEMPLATION

Other people just seem unreasonable sometimes – they just don't want to work in the same way as us and make us feel unhappy by engaging in arguments or challenging opinion. It's easy to become angry and emotional.

APPLICATION

I need to check myself when others are getting upset with me. I need to make an effort to check and then change my reactions constantly so that I am able to move as the demands of people and time change. This will bring about true contentment – such contentment that neither will I be upset nor will I upset others.

DAY 192

VALUE: FAITH

"The one who has faith is able to vanquish negativity."

CONTEMPLATION

Whenever we encounter a challenge, we tend to lose faith in our ability to find a resolution. Although we have the resources to work on the problem at hand, we are unaware of them.

APPLICATION

To vanquish negativity, I need to strengthen my faith in myself. If I focus on one thought such as, "I am victorious," I will find that all negative thoughts are lifted. Whenever I channel my faith into a powerful positive thought, there is no room for negativity.

DAY 193

VALUE: POWER

"To have power is to be able to change a problem into a solution."

CONTEMPLATION

It is easy to look for excuses and find reasons not to solve a problem. But we are aware that this is not the right solution. When we are honest with ourselves, we know we are not happy with the situation, but somehow we either do not or cannot find a way out.

APPLICATION

The key to dealing with the problems life throws at me is learning that rather than trying to change a situation I don't like, I can empower myself in order to deal with it more easily. When I learn how to use the power within me, I find solutions to problems much more easily.

DAY 194

VALUE: VIRTUE

"To admire or to praise someone's virtues is to emulate them."

CONTEMPLATION

When we notice someone's unique qualities, we begin to admire them and talk about them to others. But although we appreciate virtues in others, we rarely make the effort to develop those qualities in ourselves.

APPLICATION

I need to understand that I appreciate particular virtues in another person because they are subtly working within me too. When I work on developing them consciously, they will emerge easily.

DAY 195

VALUE: POSITIVITY

"To be free from worry means having the power to change negative into positive."

CONTEMPLATION

It is easy to worry about something when it doesn't work out according to our expectations. We become unable to think rationally, and the solution becomes buried in a mound of worry.

APPLICATION

When I am free from worry, I am able to focus on finding a solution immediately instead of focusing on the problem itself. This internal silence gives a feeling of power, which transforms me in a second and only the goodness is absorbed.

Day 196

Value: Inner transformation

"By transforming the self you transform the world."

Contemplation

Sometimes we rage that everything is wrong in the world –
there are wars and terrible crimes against humanity and our
environment – and yet nothing we do makes a difference.

Application

Today I will think about this: when I change myself, the world
around me starts to change. If I approach every situation and
person with love and humility, those characteristics change the
situations and people I come into contact with for the better.
And the waves of positive change continue out into the world. I
will show others the example of my self-transformation.

DAY 197

VALUE: COURAGE

"A single courageous step brings much progress."

CONTEMPLATION

Often when we encounter a difficult situation we become afraid. At the time we need courage most, we are filled with fear and anxiety. These feelings deplete our energy and we find it difficult to do anything to change the situation.

APPLICATION

When I understand how much potential I truly have, I find the courage to take one step forward. With each step taken with courage, there is a hundred-fold help received. When I face my fears and step forward courageously, I am able to make a lot of progress.

DAY 198

VALUE: INFLUENCE

"The way to influence others is through my own talents."

CONTEMPLATION

When we want to make an impact on people, we usually try and exert our authority over them in a negative way, either through words or through our attitude. People may respond initially, but after a while, we find they stop responding to us positively any more.

APPLICATION

The only way to create a positive impact on others is to use my unique talents. I need to recognize my own special qualities and use them in my interactions with others. This will automatically influence people in a positive way, and I will then never need to use my authority in a negative way.

Day 199

Value: Determination

"The one who is determined to succeed will find a way."

Contemplation

Often we find ourselves blaming situations and people for what is happening in our lives. We express the wish to do something to change the situation, but at the same time we find excuses to do nothing.

Application

The real solution lies in first seeing what the situation demands from me. Whatever the present situation is, it has come to me for a reason. So when I stop making excuses, I start thinking of a way to use my talents to find a way to succeed.

Day 200

Value: Self-Control

"To be a master is to be able to experience freedom."

Contemplation

Usually when things go wrong we find ourselves caught up with weaknesses. We give in to them and find ourselves totally bound. This in turn makes us feel as heavy as we feel helpless. If this continues we will never be able to overcome our weaknesses.

Application

I need to remind myself of my powers and the fact that my weakness is my own creation and I am its master. The more I remind myself of this, the more I will be able to experience freedom and use these powers. Then I'll enjoy freedom, whatever the situation.

DAY 201

VALUE: KNOWLEDGE

"To recognize the worth of the jewels of knowledge is to use them well."

CONTEMPLATION

Normally, when we know something that is not applicable in our lives right now, we tend either to ignore it or to think of it only as a theoretical viewpoint. We do not understand the worth of that jewel of knowledge and so are unable to use it enrich our lives.

APPLICATION

Each and every new point that I hear and read about is interesting. Knowledge is not only theory, but can be translated into practical action. The more I learn, the better equipped I will be to deal with whatever situations I face in the future.

DAY 202

VALUE: FORGIVENESS

"To forgive means to forget the negativity of the past."

CONTEMPLATION

When someone does something wrong toward us, we tend to hold on to that in the form of negative attitudes. As we are unable to forget it, it continues to influence all future interactions with that person. Even if the other person manages to change, our negative attitude toward him makes it difficult for him to sustain his change.

APPLICATION

I need to develop the power to forgive and forget other people's mistakes and remember their positive actions. By creating a positive environment, I make it easier for others to overcome their weaknesses and realize their potential.

Day 203

Value: Responsibility

"To be responsible at all times is to be constantly accurate."

Contemplation

Very often we find ourselves leaving things to chance or to others. We tend to take care of the big stuff and become careless about the little items. When we leave things for others to take care of they may not do them, then we become disappointed – even if we have not officially delegated the tasks to them.

Application

When I recognize that I am fully responsible for the task at hand, and that I need to oversee both the big things and the little items, I will stop being careless. I'll make a point of taking care of every aspect to the end. This will bring accuracy to my tasks and will also enable me to delegate well.

DAY 204

VALUE: DISCERNMENT

"To be free from seeing weaknesses is to be in constant peace."

CONTEMPLATION

We experience a lack of peace when we become aware of others' weaknesses. Once we have noticed someone's weaknesses, we find it difficult to ignore them. We know that we can do nothing to change others. Whatever is out of our control creates stress.

APPLICATION

Trying to focus on other people's talents and positive traits helps free me from seeing only their weaknesses. The more I connect with others and appreciate their unique gifts and talents, the more able I am to help them develop. In this way, I create a positive environment for everyone's personal growth.

DAY 205

VALUE: BALANCE

"To serve with the balance of the head and the heart is to be
constantly successful."

CONTEMPLATION

When we work only with our heart, success is fleeting. But if
we work only with the head, relying on logical thinking, we get
the task done but somehow the beauty is missing.

APPLICATION

To be successful throughout life, I need to balance love with
logical thinking. When I think with my heart as well as my
head, I become balanced. I am then better able to see all the
options available to me, which will lead to greater success.

DAY 206

VALUE: FAITH

"The one who has faith is the one who is always happy."

CONTEMPLATION

When we have faith, happiness is visible in everything we do. Whatever obstacles come our way, faith gives us the confidence to overcome them. We are able to stay constantly happy because with faith we see things clearly and do not lose heart.

APPLICATION

In any task I take up, I need to keep telling myself that I will to succeed, whatever difficulties I must face. This constant reminder gives me the faith to go on with happiness.

DAY 207

VALUE: PATIENCE

"A long-term practice brings long-term gain."

CONTEMPLATION

When we put in effort we expect to experience permanent gain through the changes we bring about. But while such effort is sincere, it generally lasts only for some time. When we expect a great deal of change from a small amount of effort, that change is usually only short-lived.

APPLICATION

If I want to achieve long-lasting change, I need to commit and put in a significant amount of effort. It is not enough to practise only when a challenging situation comes up. It is more important to practise sufficiently so that I am ready prepared to face problems whenever they arise. This type of practice over a long period brings a long-term result.

Day 208

Value: Generosity

"Generosity brings contentment."

Contemplation

It is natural to share our resources with others. Yet when we give something we are not free from expectation. We tend to look for others' co-operation to match what we have given. But we do not always get from others as we have given. Disappointment follows.

Application

True generosity brings contentment. I need to appreciate the fact that there is joy in giving. When I am able to enjoy the act of giving, that itself becomes a source of income and I am then not caught up with expectations of what I would get. To give means to appreciate what I have and to share it with others.

DAY 209

VALUE: CLARITY

"The one whose vision is clear is the one who is successful."

CONTEMPLATION

Even when we have a fixed goal in mind, it is easy to get distracted by other things going on around us. Even a small negative or positive incident is enough to distract our thoughts. We are sometimes so busy that our vision becomes clouded and we stop moving forward.

APPLICATION

I need to visualize what I want to achieve, and keep reminding myself of this until I reach my goal. By focusing only on what is important to achieve the task, I will achieve success quickly and not be distracted by other, unimportant things.

DAY 210

VALUE: PATIENCE

"To have determination is to have the patience to wait for the fruits of one's labors."

CONTEMPLATION

When we take up something new, we are determined and we want to give our best to the end. But often we grow bored and move on to something new before we have really given the first option a chance. The more this happens, the harder it is for us to succeed.

APPLICATION

When I begin to do something, along with determination I also need patience. Patience helps me to wait and watch calmly for the fruit of my effort to be seen. Determination gives me the ability to go on planting new seeds of effort knowing the fruit is sure to come. And so there is never failure, but only a journey toward success.

DAY 211

VALUE: FLEXIBILITY

"The one who knows to adjust is the one who knows how to survive."

CONTEMPLATION

Often when we have to adjust to a person or a situation, we experience many negative thoughts. We find it difficult and tend to feel that we are making this adjustment only for the other person's benefit.

APPLICATION

To adjust means to understand that nothing can be done to change a situation – it is more sensible to accept it. I adjust not because it will benefit others, but because I will benefit in the long run. This is like crossing a physical obstacle: I cannot remove it, so I have to find a way around it if I am to progress.

DAY 212

VALUE: WISDOM

"To be prepared for the tests of life is to be wise."

CONTEMPLATION

We usually prepare for the tests of life only after being faced with them. Then although we try hard, we are unable to make full preparations and find it difficult to experience progress. To anticipate and be well-prepared beforehand is to use inner resources well.

APPLICATION

In order to move forward constantly, I need to be prepared well in advance. I can only do this when I keep learning from all my past experiences. With this inner preparation I can face all life's tests. I have all the weapons I need to deal with the present situation.

Day 213

Value: Discernment

"To appreciate the drama of life is to be in constant joy."

Contemplation

Each day we begin with an expectation that everything should go smoothly. We don't really want anything to go wrong, and if it does, we are attacked with a storm of negative thoughts. Such thoughts can stop us from enjoying the rest of the day.

Application

I need to understand that the drama of life is beautiful. Each day is different and has something special to offer me. When I learn to appreciate that each day is unique, I am able to enjoy whatever comes my way.

DAY 214

VALUE: INTROSPECTION

"To think better is to find solutions."

CONTEMPLATION

When we are faced with problems we try hard to find a solution. If the solution isn't easily found, we tend to think harder. We dwell on the problem at hand and our thinking becomes circular. The more thoughts we have, the less able we are to reach a solution.

APPLICATION

In order to find solutions to problems, it is important to improve the quality of my thinking. I need to calm my mind by creating peaceful thoughts. The first thing that follows is that problems stop affecting me. I am able to think more clearly, which brings about a solution.

DAY 215

VALUE: TRUTH

"To experience truth is to bring it to life."

CONTEMPLATION

When we hear something new and worthwhile, we naturally want to incorporate it into our life. But the urge to put it into practice is soon forgotten. After a while, we remember it only as a theory and no longer feel inspired by it. We do not have the courage to put it into practice, or we find ourselves disheartened by past experience.

APPLICATION

When I want to bring something new into my life, I need to make space for it. When I imagine what my life would be like if I could make the change, I begin to bring it to life. Gradually my courage grows. The truth makes me strong and powerful, and I am successful in changing my life in a way that truly benefits me.

DAY 216

VALUE: SIMPLICITY

"To be simple is to be truly royal."

CONTEMPLATION

Simplicity is usually considered as plain, with no decoration. So when we think of simplicity we are often not so attracted toward it. We tend to make a lot of effort to make ourselves seem fascinating to others. But in the process we lose touch with our innate purity and innocence and become unable to express our true beauty.

APPLICATION

Simplicity means complete purity. It is to be egoless and free from every kind of negativity. So when I return to my natural simplicity I become able to express my innate beauty and strength.

Day 217

Value: Self-control

"True control means mastery of the self."

Contemplation

We usually look for order in external situations. We want everything to be logical and to follow our notion of right and wrong. When it doesn't happen that way, we tend to get disturbed. We are not able to keep our mind under control. This can make a negative situation worse, and makes it difficult to find a solution to the problem

Application

When I respect myself and realize my potential I am able to control my mind. Like a king rules his kingdom, I rule myself. This helps me to keep external situations under control. It also enables me to see the order behind everything that is happening, so I do not become upset.

DAY 218

VALUE: PEACE

"To experience peace is to give others the experience of peace."

CONTEMPLATION

When we lack a sense of peace, we generally blame others. We think that the other person or situation has made us lose our cool. Even though we don't like this state of mind, we don't make much effort to change it. Our own discontentment means that those around us also experience peacelessness.

APPLICATION

To change the situation, I first need to work out why I feel a lack of peace. When I have solved my inner conflict, I will become calm once more, and will be able to share this experience with others.

Day 219

Value: Contentment

"The one with contentment is neither upset nor upsets others."

Contemplation

Many times I find that my words, actions or behavior tend to upset others even though I don't want to hurt them. I seem to be very happy with the situation, but others are not. At that time I am not really able to understand the reason and I consider the others to be unreasonable.

Application

I need to check myself when others are getting upset with me. I need to make the effort to check and change myself constantly so that I can move along with the demands of time. This will bring about true contentment – such contentment that neither will I be upset nor will I upset others.

DAY 220

VALUE: HAPPINESS

"The one who is happy with themselves can make others happy too."

CONTEMPLATION

Most of our time goes into pleasing others and making them happy. Often, despite our best efforts, we find that people do not appreciate what we have done. When we have tried hard to please someone, we feel disheartened and upset.

APPLICATION

Whatever I do is for myself. When I recognize this fact, I will never do anything just to please others. When I am content with the effort I put in, I will never be dependent on others' recognition of what I have done. When I enjoy everything I do, I will be truly happy. The more content I am, the more others will start appreciating my effort.

Day 221

Value: Courage

"To receive help, we must first have courage."

Contemplation

When we become involved in something difficult, we often to look for help from people even before we have started. If the help we seek does not arrive immediately, we tend to get disheartened and maybe even give up trying altogether.

Application

Before I can receive help from others, I need to have the courage to help myself. When I take the first step toward my goal, I will find that others come forward to help me. I will never need to ask for help, but will find that it comes automatically, often in an unexpected way.

Day 222

Value: Self-control

"To control oneself is to have everything in control."

Contemplation

When things go wrong, our first thought is often about controlling the situations or people involved. But since neither the situations nor people are in our hands, there is no success guaranteed with this way of thinking. Which only increases the negativity.

Application

Instead of trying to control something I have no control upon, I need to start with myself. The more I am able to control myself with constant attention, checking and changing, the more I will have everything under control.

Day 223

Value: Determination

"Determination brings success."

Contemplation

During the difficult phases we tend to experience a lot of negativity within. That particular situation then seems awfully big, and it also seems to last forever.

Application

I need to recognize that difficulties are not a huge as they might initially seem. And that though time seems to stand still, it is moving on – and every new minute brings a renewed opportunity for change and success. I need to develop the determination to work on my problems with this understanding. I will then be able to face any situation with ease.

DAY 224

VALUE: FLEXIBILITY

"A flying bird crosses all problems."

CONTEMPLATION

Problems seem like huge burdens when they are on top of us, and overwhelm our ability to act and move forward.

APPLICATION

If I think of myself as like a bird in the air, I can swoop up above my problems and look down on them. They might still be down there, but up here I am free. Having a mind this flexible is the solution to all problems.

DAY 225

VALUE: INTROVERSION

"Being free from bondage to the material world brings liberation."

CONTEMPLATION

Being extroverted leads to wasteful thoughts – they become attached to things that can never bring us happiness. Possessions will inevitably break and even friendships may break down, leading to sadness and regret.

APPLICATION

The only way to real happiness and a sense of liberation is in looking for happiness, peace and power within. All this sweetness, which I have been looking for outside myself all these years is in fact inside – and today I will start looking for it.

DAY 226

VALUE: HAPPINESS

"To be happy is to spread rays of happiness throughout the world."

CONTEMPLATION

When we are truly happy we embody happiness in such a way that our happiness spreads out like rays of sunshine throughout the world, helping other to experience a little of our bliss.

APPLICATION

I must not just speak of happiness, I must experience it. Then I will embody it in a way that transfers to others and transforms their lives, too.

DAY 227

VALUE: CHANGE

"To change one's attitude is to change the world."

CONTEMPLATION

When we have a problem in a particular relationship, we are not able to think about that person in a positive way. Our negative attitude creates an atmosphere of negativity, which becomes difficult to get rid of. This makes the relationship and the situation become worse.

APPLICATION

The only way to improve a relationship is to create a positive environment by changing my own attitude toward that person. This silent change within creates a positive impact on people through subtle vibrations. By adjusting my attitude, I create a more beautiful world for myself and others, where my presence has a positive impact on people.

DAY 228

VALUE: HAPPINESS

"True happiness lies within the self."

CONTEMPLATION

In negative situations, we tend to search for happiness outside ourselves. We either try to find a temporary source of happiness to take our mind off a problem, or we try to move away from that situation. Neither approach helps us to solve the problem.

APPLICATION

To find true happiness, I need to find what really nourishes my spirit and gives me life. When I find my inner source of happiness, it will remain stable and unchanging even in the most chaotic conditions.

DAY 229

VALUE: POSITIVITY

"To change the focus from negative to positive is to create hope."

CONTEMPLATION

We are becoming more pessimistic with each passing day, as negativity surrounds us on all sides. Our normal conversations and interactions are full of negativity, whether we are aware of this or not. So without our conscious knowledge, we develop a negative approach to life.

APPLICATION

It is important for me to be aware when my conversations with others become negative. I need to make a conscious change to start being more positive, and appreciate what life gives me. So much good in my life goes unnoticed. When I focus on the positive it creates an environment of enthusiasm for the future that affects everyone around me.

DAY 230

VALUE: LETTING GO

"To be free from expectations is to be free from sorrow."

CONTEMPLATION

When someone does something that contradicts our expectations, we may try to change them according to what we feel is right. Of course, they will resist our effort, and this engenders sorrow.

APPLICATION

When I see someone behaving differently to what I expect, I need to understand that this person is a unique individual. He will behave according to what he understands at any given moment. I cannot expect him to act in a particular way. By letting go of my expectations I am freed from sorrow.

DAY 231

VALUE: RESPECT

"To have respect for everyone is to have self-control."

CONTEMPLATION

We sometimes feel the need to exert our authority over others and demand their respect. But respect that is not freely given is not true respect. We soon find that we have no control over others or their behavior, and little is achieved.

APPLICATION

The best way to get things done is to respect everyone and acknowledge that we all have unique gifts and talents. When I respect others, they also respect me. This mutual respect helps us to understand each other, and allows us to work together for everyone's benefit.

DAY 232

VALUE: DETACHMENT

"Being a detached observer makes heroes of us."

CONTEMPLATION

Obstacles or difficulties arise when we become attached to particular ways of behaving or understanding.

APPLICATION

If I am to succeed I must think of myself as a detached observer. This means detaching from my body and listening instead to my soul. The soul is my best guide and will show me how to become a hero. I will let it be my master.

DAY 233

VALUE: HAPPINESS

"May you embody your attainments."

CONTEMPLATION

The face reveals all the difficulties we face everyday – every frown line is a sign of the attitude we bring to our relations with the world and those around us.

APPLICATION

I will let my face express my spiritual attainments today – my peace, happiness, knowledge and joy. When the sparkle of all this spiritual wealth is visible to all, everyone benefits.

Day 234

Value: Courage

"Sometimes being courageous means accepting help from others."

Contemplation

When we are faced with more demands than we are used to, fear grows, and we find ourselves unable to face a situation. Then the powers within us remain hidden beneath the fear.

Application

When I begin to be aware of and appreciate the resources I have within, I become able to access them and put them to use. This takes courage. But then others will automatically be drawn to my aid and I will find myself in a better position than I was.

DAY 235

VALUE: SWEETNESS

"To recognize truth is to experience sweetness."

CONTEMPLATION

When something negative happens that negativity tends to color our thinking. We do not see the situation clearly, and may overlook positive aspects hidden beneath the bad things.

APPLICATION

To recognize the truth is to enable beauty to emerge from every word and action. Truth allows me to appreciate my innate nature. In turn, this helps me to bring sweetness to everything I do, however difficult or challenging the situation might be.

DAY 236

VALUE: POSITIVITY

"Positive thoughts equip others with the power to succeed."

CONTEMPLATION

We often end up doing too much for others in an effort to help them. Sometimes the best way to help someone is by thought alone and not by deed.

APPLICATION

Today I will fill myself with positive thoughts. These will quite naturally extend out toward all those I would like to help. When I spread positive vibrations through my mind in this way, I help others to help themselves so they learn to become successful without constantly relying on support from others.

DAY 237

VALUE: COMMUNICATION

"The one who knows the art of connecting to others is successful."

CONTEMPLATION

When someone is not behaving well, we tend to alter our attitude, response and behavior toward that person. We wait for the other person to change, before changing ourselves. So neither do we find change in others nor in ourselves.

APPLICATION

When I know the art of perceiving others' specialties and connecting to them, I will always be successful. I am then not dependent on the other person's behavior for my own growth. I am able to see each person's positive aspects and absorb them in myself too. Then I become richer with every interaction.

DAY 238

VALUE: LETTING GO

"The one who has the ability to 'let go' is able to experience success."

CONTEMPLATION

"Letting go" is usually thought of as losing out. If we let go of something, it is perceived as "giving up". Letting go can be a positive experience, but letting go without understanding leads to second thoughts and feelings of dissatisfaction.

APPLICATION

I need to understand what I have to gain by letting go: I learn something new from the situation. When I take the opportunity to bring about a change in myself, I experience progress. I don't try to control a situation or another person but instead enjoy learning at every step. By letting go, I am able to take control.

Day 239

Value: Learning from mistakes

"To learn means to bring about a practical change."

Contemplation

There are often important lessons in the situations we put ourselves into everyday. But sometimes we find ourselves making the same mistakes over and again. Although we have understood, we are not able to bring about real change from the experience.

Application

Once I realize a mistake, I need to spend some time contemplating it. Today I will think back to situations in the recent past and ask myself why they happened, what I understand about them now, and what will stop me from making the same mistake in the future. This analysis will help me to bring about real change.

DAY 240

VALUE: INNER STRENGTH

"To be free from weaknesses is to move forward constantly."

CONTEMPLATION

Most of the time we manage to defeat our weaknesses and achieve progress. But sometimes we find that we are overcome by our weaknesses and find ourselves moving backward.

APPLICATION

In order to benefit others and myself, I need to seek out the last trace of weakness working within me. When I find the real cause of the weakness, I can then remove it. By constantly working to overcome my weaknesses in this way, I become strong and able to progress.

DAY 241

VALUE: APPRECIATION

"To appreciate one's resources brings constant progress."

CONTEMPLATION

It is much easier to note what we are lacking than appreciate what we have. Whenever challenging situations come our way, we tend focus on only what we are lacking. When we have this attitude, we are unable to make any effort to change the situation. We then tend to blame others or give excuses.

APPLICATION

I need to make special effort to appreciate and use the gifts I have been given. Today I will treat every challenge as an opportunity to develop my skills and discover my hidden resources. The more I do this, the more progress I will make.

DAY 242

VALUE: DISCERNMENT

"Those with the right attitude make the best contribution."

CONTEMPLATION

Sometimes although an act in itself is right, we find that the result lacks something. When this happens, it can be difficult to understand why things haven't turned out better. We find ourselves questioning everything, without finding the answer. This creates a negative attitude toward the situation and people involved.

APPLICATION

I need to think about the motive behind my actions. If I have the right attitude, it becomes a powerful seed, which will eventually bear fruit at the proper time. All other situations will then nurture this seed instead of creating obstacles or further misunderstanding.

DAY 243

VALUE: SELFLESSNESS

"Selflessness brings happiness."

CONTEMPLATION

When there is selfishness there is always a desire. Because of this desire we are unable to experience satisfaction. We always want more than what we are able to get. When we remain focused on our own desires, we are unable to become a giver, or to share resources for others' benefit. Until we learn to give we cannot be truly happy.

APPLICATION

When I am selfless I have respect for my own resources and I am able to use them for everyone's benefit. I have the satisfaction of using what I have, without expecting others to appreciate me. I become a giver instead of a taker, which brings constant happiness.

Day 244

Value: Flexibility

"To know the art of being flexible is to create beauty in one's life."

Contemplation

Sometimes we become stuck in our ways. We are all individuals, and do things according to our own personality, custom and desire. But to appreciate the beauty of life, we need to understand that there are different ways of doing things. When we are flexible, we can learn a lot from what others have to teach us.

Application

The real art of flexibility lies in appreciating everyone as an individual. This appreciation brings about natural respect for others. When I value others as unique individuals I don't expect them to mold themselves according to my desires. Instead, I am able to learn from them, and their perspective on the world.

DAY 245

VALUE: HAPPINESS

"The nourishment of happiness keeps one healthy."

CONTEMPLATION

To be truly happy means not relying on external stimuli for happiness, but discovering the joy within. Someone who is in touch with the happiness within them is able to express it in all areas of their life. Happiness leads to healthiness – when we are happy, we are also free from illnesses affecting the body.

APPLICATION

I am able to enjoy the beauty of everything when I maintain my own inner state of happiness. My mind, body and relationships are healthy because of this state of mind. I am able to enjoy everything I do too and experience constant progress.

DAY 246

VALUE: RESPONSIBILITY

"True responsibility brings inner lightness and joy."

CONTEMPLATION

When we are responsible for something or someone, we tend to feel burdened or trapped by the person or situation. When we feel handicapped in this way, work is not done in the best way possible.

APPLICATION

The true meaning of responsibility is not just duties to be done, but has more to do with being honest to the task and doing everything with a sense of purpose. When I work with this attitude I find things getting easier and I receive help at every step. I am able to accomplish more work with more lightness and enjoy all I do.

DAY 247

VALUE: DETACHMENT

"Even challenges are a game for the one who is detached."

CONTEMPLATION

When we are detached we do not become emotionally involved
in a situation. Detachment helps us remain calm in difficult
circumstances, rather than becoming disturbed or confused. It
gives us the power to observe any situation, no matter how
difficult, just as we would observe a game.

APPLICATION

In any situation in which I feel helpless, I need to develop the
power of detachment. I should practise looking at the situation
as I would watch a play. Then I can feel light and enjoy the
different turns that the plot takes. I no longer feel trapped by
the circumstances I find myself in; instead I am able to address
them rationally.

DAY 248

VALUE: APPRECIATION

"To appreciate the worth of every individual is to become worthwhile."

CONTEMPLATION

We tend to measure our worth on our achievement or how much people appreciate us. This makes us dependent on the external environment for our self-worth. Since what comes from outside is not always stable, we find ourselves fluctuating in our thoughts. Sometimes we are happy and sometimes we are not.

APPLICATION

I need to understand that each and every individual has his own unique set of capabilities. When I am able to appreciate my own inherent worth I can use my skills and talents to the best of my ability. I will realize how capable I am, and no longer need affirmation from others to feel good about myself.

DAY 249

VALUE: GIVING

"To experience the innate qualities is to be a giver."

CONTEMPLATION

Whenever someone we care about deceives us, we feel disappointed, and tend to get disheartened. When this happens, positive feelings can be lost. We find ourselves rejecting the person who has hurt us, and move away from them – often physically and always mentally.

APPLICATION

If my exchanges with others are based on falsehood – on what is not connected with the innate truth – then I will find it difficult to be a giver. When I have faith in myself I learn to love myself. This love puts me in touch with my innate qualities. Thus my thoughts and feelings are pure. Then I have powerful good wishes for others and these good feelings reach them.

DAY 250

VALUE: SELF-BELIEF

"To believe in oneself means to make best use of opportunities."

CONTEMPLATION

We tend to make a lot of excuses for not doing things. We say, "if only…" or "some other time". Even if we have the ability to do something, we find some reason not to. We don't make best use of our time or our talents, which stops us fulfilling our potential.

APPLICATION

Whenever a situation demands something which I feel is beyond my capability, I need to tell myself that the circumstances have come my way as an opportunity for me to develop. When I believe in myself, I learn to see every situation as an opportunity.

DAY 251

VALUE: FLEXIBILITY

"With humility and love, flexibility becomes natural."

CONTEMPLATION

In order to be flexible we need to have the virtue of humility. With humility, we become willing to understand those around us and their behavior. Understanding brings love. When we learn to love someone, we automatically become flexible and willing to accept them as they are.

APPLICATION

When I come across someone who is not being co-operative, I need to become humble and try to understand what the other person is communicating, if not through words, then through their actions. When I am able to listen with love and understanding, I will no longer be rigid but able to adapt and support them however I can.

DAY 252

VALUE: POSITIVITY

"The power of positivity vanquishes the darkness of negativity."

CONTEMPLATION

Challenging situations tend to affect our state of mind for the worst. We often find ourselves sowing seeds of fear, worry, tension and anxiety. Those feelings grow, and soon we find ourselves feeling negative, even when we are not faced with immediate difficulties.

APPLICATION

The only way we can vanquish darkness is with light. The powerful rays of light drive out the last trace of darkness. To get rid of the negative emotions and fear that lurks in the darkness, I need to seek out my inner light. When I find the peace and power within me, I can make even negative situations positive.

DAY 253

VALUE: HAPPINESS

"To recognize the significance of challenging situations is to remain in constant happiness."

CONTEMPLATION

When difficult situations come our way, we are bound to lose our internal state of happiness. When we do not have the resources to deal with the situations we encounter, we start to think of ourselves as weak. Our mood, thoughts, words and actions become negative, and we blame this on the negativity of the situation.

APPLICATION

I need to realize that I can hold on to my inner happiness, no matter what situation I find myself in. Difficult situations arise to make me stronger and stable. I need to make an effort to recognize and experience my internal strength, so that situations don't change my mood, even temporarily. Then I will live in constant happiness, whatever the situation.

DAY 254

VALUE: SELF-CONTROL

"Words are effective only when matched with action."

CONTEMPLATION

It is far easier for us to see the mistakes of others, since we are detached from the situation. We want to help, and frequently offer advice about how to handle a situation. Once we've given our opinion, we expect others to follow our advice and bring about a change immediately. But people don't change that easily – they lack something they need to make the change happen.

APPLICATION

Before I give advice to others, I need to think about whether I actually put what I am saying into practice in my own life. Only when I follow the advice I give others will my words be effective. When I lead by example, I will inspire others to do the same.

DAY 255

VALUE: GENEROSITY

"To consider oneself to be big is to have a generous heart."

CONTEMPLATION

When we consider ourselves to be big, we usually expect from others. We want others to give respect and be obedient to whatever we say. But we do not always find others listening to us or obeying us. We are then disappointed and try to use more of our authority in a forceful way.

APPLICATION

To be big means not expecting to take but instead being a giver. If I am big I also need the understanding that I am in a better position than the other person and so I need to give. This attitude will help me gain others' good wishes – which will help me progress and continue to achieve success.

DAY 256

VALUE: CLARITY

"To see things as they are is to be free from the influence of weaknesses."

CONTEMPLATION

Sometimes we find ourselves reacting strongly when faced with small upsets. We may try to change such negative feelings, but sometimes are not able to, either because of our personality as a whole or the personality trait we are working with at that time.

APPLICATION

If I have to change my reactions to the situations that I am faced with, I need to change the way I see things. I need to understand the situation as it is and not let it be colored by my own personality traits. When I see things as they are, I am able to act in situations instead of reacting.

Day 257

Value: Determination

"Determination overcomes weaknesses."

Contemplation

We all have weaknesses. But a determined thought is all we need to overcome them. When we become determined, the influence of others' carelessness will not affect us. Once the seed of determination has been sown, it will grow within us and begin to have a positive effect on those around us.

Application

Determination will help me overcome my weaknesses, one step at a time. A single determined thought will start my march toward victory. Today, if I see others with the same weakness, I will not let it affect my determination to overcome that weakness in myself. I will make sure I don't fall into the trap of making excuses, too. Instead, I will remind myself of my goal and keep working until I achieve success.

DAY 258

VALUE: COURAGE

"Success is achieved when courage is combined with understanding."

CONTEMPLATION

Courage helps us face our fears and take on new challenges. But sometimes we think we are being courageous when we leap into the unknown without stopping to consider the consequences. When we combine courage with knowledge and understanding we experience greater success. Knowledge gives us the ability to discriminate, helping us to try something new without taking unwanted risks.

APPLICATION

Before I start something new, I need to consider if what I am doing is right. I also need to think carefully about the consequences of my actions. When I am sure this is the right course of action, courage will help me achieve success.

DAY 259

VALUE: GIVING

"To help others discover their talents is the best help we can give."

CONTEMPLATION

Sometimes people are unaware of their talents, or afraid to use them. But if we do not use the gifts we have been given, we can never be truly happy. Throughout our lives, people help us grow. As we grow older, we realize we can help others, too.

APPLICATION

Making others aware of the things they do well and subtly encouraging them to use their talents is the best way to help them progress. Because I am detached from their lives, it is easier for me to be objective and offer constructive advice. I do not seek any reward for helping them, but instead experience the joy of watching their talents blossom.

DAY 260

VALUE: RESPECT

"To have respect is to appreciate another's commitment to change."

CONTEMPLATION

Usually we want people to change in a way that suits us. So when we see someone behaving differently to what we expect, we tend to react negatively and try to prove them wrong. Although we think we have their best interests at heart, this often isn't the case.

APPLICATION

When I have respect for another person, I recognize and support their commitment to change. I will be able to give them the guidance they need, without taking over or steering them in a particular direction. I will help to inspire change instead of forcing things on others. Gradually, I will find it easier to accept change in others.

DAY 261

VALUE: FAITH

"Faith that things will turn out for the best leads to enjoyment of whatever life brings."

CONTEMPLATION

Throughout the day we encounter numerous situations that seem difficult. But if we have faith that everything happens for a reason, we will be able to enjoy each and every moment. When we believe that things will turn out for the best, we will be able to take something positive from every situation we encounter, and we will learn from our mistakes.

APPLICATION

It is good practice to end each day by reflecting on what went wrong throughout the day and what I have learnt from the mistakes I made. When I am sure that I have learnt something, I will understand that whatever has happened was for my own good.

DAY 262

VALUE: APPRECIATION

"Only when we appreciate our fortune will be able to use it
effectively."

CONTEMPLATION

The more we appreciate the fortune we have attained, the more
we will enjoy sharing it with others. When we share our riches
with others, the more we find that they come back to us.

APPLICATION

We are blessed with virtues and talents. I need to think of all the
ways in which I consider myself fortunate. When I learn to
appreciate them, I will stop expecting something more. Then I
will be able to make the best use of what I have and start to focus
on using my fortune for the benefit of others as well as myself.

Day 263

Value: Courage

"The sign of courage is never to be defeated."

Contemplation

During difficult situations if our thoughts, words or actions become negative, we will be defeated. When we draw on our courage, we make our thoughts, words or actions powerful, and will always be victorious. Difficult situations will always arise, but as long as we have courage, we will achieve success.

Application

I need to remind myself that courage will help me face any difficulties I encounter. Today I will look back at all my past achievements and realize just how much I am capable of. This will strengthen my faith in myself, and in my ability to find the best solution for the problem at hand.

DAY 264

VALUE: DETACHMENT

"True detachment is to use everything but to remain beyond its influence."

CONTEMPLATION

Throughout the day we use a lot of resources in the outside world, which often helps make our lives easier. We do not need to stop ourselves from using them. But if we can use them without becoming dependent on them, we can say we are truly detached. That means we can use everything available to us, but as a means of supporting our inner resources, rather than replacing them.

APPLICATION

In order to be happy in all circumstances, I need to practise remaining detached. If there is a time when I have no external support, I can remain happy. Because I have the power of detachment, I don't become dependent on anything or anyone else.

Day 265

Value: Being Present

"To make the most of the present is to use it well."

Contemplation

When things go wrong, we often wait for the difficult time to pass so that we can return to our normal schedule. But this only makes us lose valuable time.

Application

In order to use time well, I need to understand the importance of being in the moment. The word "present" has more than one meaning. We can think of it as "this moment", the immediate moment in time. It can also mean a gift. When we think of time as a gift that is given to us, it immediately takes on more significance. It becomes something that we treasure and want to make the most of.

Day 266

Value: Determination

"True determination is a combination of single-mindedness and flexibility."

Contemplation

When we are sure of what we need to achieve, we are able to move toward it. When we find an obstacle in our way, we are able to take it in our stride. Like a river cuts its own path through the land, each of us is able to create our own route toward our destination.

Application

Every morning, I need to choose one thing I want to achieve. Throughout the day I need to keep reminding myself of my aim. This will help me make sure that I am moving in the right direction and that I don't stop even if there are obstacles in my way.

DAY 267

VALUE: FAITH

"The one who has faith is the one who is always happy."

CONTEMPLATION

When we have faith, happiness is visible in our every thought, word and action. Whatever obstacles come our way, faith in the self brings the confidence to face them. Faith also helps us see problems clearly. Because we believe we can overcome the problem, we see it as it really is, rather than letting negative reactions distort the situation. This helps us remain happy no matter what we have to deal with.

APPLICATION

In any task I take up, I need to remind myself that I will succeed, regardless of the problems I have to face. This constant reminder strengthens my faith to continue, and I proceed with happiness.

Day 268

Value: Forgiveness

"To seek forgiveness means never repeating mistakes."

Contemplation

To seek forgiveness from someone means that we have realized we've made a mistake. It is to make a promise that we will never commit that mistake again. Once we have understood where we have gone wrong, we try hard to ensure that we never repeat the mistake.

Application

When I have to apologize to someone for some mistake that I have made, I need to pay special attention to make sure I never repeat that mistake. I need to reflect on where I went wrong to help me understand where I went wrong and how I can learn from it. I also need to forgive myself for making the mistake.

DAY 269

VALUE: FLEXIBILITY

"Habits break easily when there is flexibility."

CONTEMPLATION

It is easy to fall into habits or ways of doing something. Sometimes these routines are helpful. But at other times they stop us seeing that there may be a better way of doing things. To achieve constant success, we need to become flexible.

APPLICATION

Habits can be hard to break. It is easier for me to hold on to an old way of doing something than to make the effort to break it. If I want to get rid of a particular habit, I have to remind myself constantly of the need to break it. I need to become flexible – to tell myself that I needn't act in the same way I have always done; instead I can think of a new way of being.

DAY 270

VALUE: DETACHMENT

"Detachment adds quality to each and every action."

CONTEMPLATION

When we are detached, we are not be bound by our actions. When we do things, we are not dependent on their result. This automatically increases the quality of the things we do.

APPLICATION

In any situation in which I find myself doing a lot yet feeling I am not achieving anything, I should question how attached I am to the task at hand. The more attached I am to a task, the more effort I put in. But often this actually means I achieve less. When I am detached I am able to give my best in all that I do.

DAY 271

VALUE: FLEXIBILITY

"With humility and love, flexibility becomes natural."

CONTEMPLATION

In order to be flexible, we need to develop the virtue of humility. With humility, we become willing to make the effort to understand those around us, and the reasons behind their behavior. When we understand them, we will also be able to love them. This naturally makes us more flexible, as well as more forgiving of others and ourselves.

APPLICATION

When I come across someone who is not being co-operative, I need to become humble and try to understand what the other person is communicating, if not through words at least through actions. When I am able to listen with love and understanding, I will not be rigid anymore, but will be able to adapt to communicate and co-operate with others.

Day 272

Value: Generosity

"The one who is generous gets everything and is yet free from desires."

Contemplation

When we are truly generous, we give what we can without any thought of getting anything in return. Without expectations, we are better able to appreciate all the good things that life brings us.

Application

When I find myself expecting something, I need to remind myself instead to think of what I can do for others. I need to learn how to let go of my expectations and have that faith that I will receive what I need at the right time. The more I am able to overcome my desires in this way, the more I find that what is right comes to me naturally.

DAY 273

VALUE: DETERMINATION

"Determination can change opposition and make things happen
in the proper way."

CONTEMPLATION

When we have faith and determination in a task we have taken
up, hurdles become opportunities. This is because we are
constantly learning and moving forward. When others become
aware of my determination to succeed, they will co-operate to
make the task successful.

APPLICATION

Each day I need to reflect on all the tasks that did not turn out
right. I need to check whether the problem was due to a lack of
determination. If so, I know that the power to solve the
problem is in my hands. To achieve my goal, I need simply to
keep my aim in mind while I am working on the task. This will
strengthen my determination and lead to success.

DAY 274

VALUE: FLEXIBILITY

"Flexibility transforms problems into lessons."

CONTEMPLATION

Flexibility equips us to learn and develop throughout life. It helps us appreciate that all the situations we come across have something to teach us, if we are willing and able to learn. When we encounter problems, instead of letting fear stop us in our tracks, we will then be able to see the positive in everything.

APPLICATION

Whenever I find myself facing a problem, I need to remind myself that the situation around me will not remain the same. Things might get worse before they get better, but that this will only be a temporary situation. If I learn how to be flexible now, I will be able to adjust to any situation I might be faced with in the future.

Day 275

Value: Forgiveness

"To forgive oneself is to move forward with lightness."

Contemplation

It is natural to make mistakes, and equally natural to feel guilty about them. This can make us feel heavy, and stops us making best use of our time. When we are caught up in the past, we are unable to engage fully with the present. So it is important to be light, without becoming careless.

Application

When I do something wrong, before I can forgive myself, I need to identify the weakness that caused me to make that mistake. When I am aware of this, I will be able to use the incident as a gift that aids my progress. I will be able to move forward with lightness.

DAY 276

VALUE: HAPPINESS

"Happiness within oneself changes hopeless situations into hopeful ones."

CONTEMPLATION

Happiness is powerful. It can help us transform our lives. Even in the most hopeless situations, our inner happiness can keep us feeling hopeful. When we are able to maintain our inner happiness, no matter what circumstances we find ourselves in, we will find that things change for the better.

APPLICATION

Today I will focus on one situation in my life that I am not happy with. I need to learn to I accept the situation as it is, without expecting it to change. This acceptance will give me the faith that things are happening for the best. With this faith even the most hopeless situation will become positive.

Day 277

Value: Forgiveness

"To forgive means to forget mistakes committed in the past."

Contemplation

To truly forgive someone for a mistake they have made, we have to be able to forget it. If we cannot, this means that we have not been able to completely forgive them. Forgiveness takes work: we have to learn to let go of the wrong done to us.

Application

When someone has done something wrong, I have to be able to look at it in a detached way. I need to remind myself that others have their own lessons to learn. If I can help them, I will. But if there is nothing I can do, I need to forget about it. I don't have to cloud my mind with negativity by thinking about it repeatedly.

DAY 278

VALUE: GENEROSITY

"To be generous-hearted is to bestow others with specialties and virtues."

CONTEMPLATION

True generosity means co-operating with others and helping them develop. Each of us has special gifts and talents that we can use to help others. When we help others nurture their own gifts, our own are allowed to blossom.

APPLICATION

I first need to think of something that is very special in me. Then I need to take the thought of using this gift for someone else's benefit each day. This thought will enable me to use my gift constantly, in a way that will benefit others as well as myself.

DAY 279

VALUE: FAITH

"Faith in the self gives us the power to face challenges."

CONTEMPLATION

When we have faith in ourselves, we will never give up. If we believe we will succeed, we can tap into our inner power to find the strength to carry on. When we believe in ourselves, we can transform negative to positive, and make the impossible possible. No challenge can stop us from moving forward.

APPLICATION

When any task demands strength beyond my capacity, I need to remind myself of the power within me. If I think back to all the times I have succeeded, despite the obstacles I faced, this will help strengthen my faith in myself and my abilities. I will then be able to face every challenge with renewed enthusiasm, knowing that I can overcome it.

DAY 280

VALUE: HAPPINESS

"Happiness is experienced by those whose actions and attitudes are pure and selfless."

CONTEMPLATION

When our actions are pure and selfless, there is no trace of negativity. Without negativity, the mind naturally becomes free from feelings of guilt, fear and sadness. We experience a constant state of happiness.

APPLICATION

If I find there is no happiness in my life, I need to reflect on what is stopping me from becoming happy. I need to think about my thoughts, words and actions, and make changes in my life which will benefit me, and those around me. When I do this, I will find that I experience constant happiness.

DAY 281

VALUE: HUMILITY

"Humility brings learning and this in turn brings progress."

CONTEMPLATION

Where there is humility, there is willingness to learn. Ego comes when humility is lacking and prevents us from learning from situations or the people around us. The power of humility equips us to learn and constantly move forward.

APPLICATION

Sometimes, things go wrong for a reason: there is a lesson we need to learn. When something goes wrong, rather than feeling bad about it, I need to see what I can learn from it. When I understand this, I will become humble. My humility helps me make sure I never become arrogant, and that I am always open to learning.

DAY 282

VALUE: GENEROSITY

"There is happiness in distributing the fruit of fortune with generosity."

CONTEMPLATION

Every one of us is blessed with unique gifts and talents. The more we understand and appreciate how fortunate we are, the more we will enjoy sharing our particular fortune with others. Whatever we share will always come back to us, and so our fortune increases.

APPLICATION

Instead of wishing I had more, or wanting something better, I need to remind myself of all the ways in which am fortunate. When I begin to appreciate what I have been given, I will be able to make the best use of what I have. This also means learning to share my fortune with others. When I do this, I will find my blessings grow naturally.

DAY 283

VALUE: PATIENCE

"Patience enables one to develop detached observation."

CONTEMPLATION

In most situations when we can do nothing about the things that are going on, we need to watch with detachment. Detachment gives us the power to wait patiently. Patience at such a time is like a protective mother who offers refuge to the child in a difficult situation just by being there.

APPLICATION

When things are not turning out well and I am unable to do anything about the situation, I need to remind myself that all I can do is wait. Patience allows me to wait for the storm to pass, and faith helps me hold on to the belief that things will get better – the clouds always lift eventually.

Day 284

Value: Simplicity

"Greatness is visible in simplicity."

Contemplation

Living a simple life helps free us from things that are
unimportant. It doesn't have to mean giving up all we have and
living an austere life. It means letting go of our attachment to
material things, rather than the things themselves.

Application

A simple lifestyle can offer inspiration to those around me. I
need to remind myself that although I do not need to give
anything up, nor should I let myself become dependent on
material objects. This allows me to become light and free. With
simplicity, my lifestyle takes on an easiness that can provide
healing and comfort to those around me.

DAY 285

VALUE: HUMILITY

"Humility brings benefit to many."

CONTEMPLATION

When we are humble, we do not do things for our own success or gratification, but for the benefit of others. Neither do we seek reward from others: to give brings its own satisfaction.

APPLICATION

Whenever I work with others, I need to learn to practice humility in order to get the best out of them and the situation. When I begin working for the greater good rather than my own benefit, I will find I am able to work with others more easily, and we achieve greater success.

DAY 286

VALUE: INTROSPECTION

"Introspection enables me to experience progress."

CONTEMPLATION

Introspection allows us to reflect upon our thoughts, words and actions. When we take the time to look within it is like holding up a mirror to our inner self. We are able to see our flaws as well as our good qualities. When we recognize our faults, we gain the power to bring about a change and achieve progress.

APPLICATION

We all have flaws, and these are what cause us to make mistakes. I need to remind myself that with each mistake I make, I actually gain a chance to learn. I can use each situation as an opportunity to progress.

DAY 287

VALUE: SILENCE

"The power of silence can bring peace to any situation."

CONTEMPLATION

The instruments for the power of silence are pure thoughts and pure feelings. When we understand and experience the power of silence, we become more powerful. As our power grows, so does our experience of peace.

APPLICATION

Silence based on pure feelings and love can help bring peace to any situation. When I have a disagreement with someone, it is far better to be silent rather than become aggressive or confrontational. When I accept other people as they are with love, I will be able to bring about a change in them. I need to remember that the less I talk, the more room I allow for peace to grow.

Day 288

Value: Stability

"The one who serves others is the one who can remain stable in all situations."

Contemplation

Serving others brings us stability. When we focus on what we can give others, rather than on what they can give us, we become grounded. We let go of our expectations of people or situations, and we attract good wishes from everyone we encounter.

Application

Each day I need to try and give something to each person I meet. This could be as simple as a good wish. The thing itself is not as important as the thought behind it. Once I learn to do this, I will be able to give continuously, whatever situation I find myself in.

DAY 289

VALUE: PATIENCE

"Patience reduces speed, which in turn, brings progress."

CONTEMPLATION

Patience makes us cool and calm. It helps us understand that like a marathon runner, it is necessary to pace ourselves and preserve our energy till the end. This naturally brings patience so that we find ourselves achieving success in everything we undertake.

APPLICATION

When I find that I am expecting too much from myself, I have to remind myself that I will achieve what I have to when I pace myself in the proper way. Trying to do too much at one time will only leave me exhausted and will achieve little. I need to learn not to rush things, but to tackle each task with care. Patience leads to greater success in the long run.

DAY 290

VALUE: HUMILITY

"Humility enables people to realize their mistakes and correct themselves."

CONTEMPLATION

Real humility results in so much power of truth that we often don't need to say anything in words. The power of our inner state of being will make other people realize the error of their ways, and will inspire them correct mistakes on their own.

APPLICATION

Only when I am humble will I be able to help others progress. I have to set an example for them to follow by making sure my thoughts, words and actions reflect those I would like to see in them. I will not need to correct others; instead, I will have the satisfaction of watching them grow.

DAY 291

VALUE: RESPECT

"Respect for the task at hand brings out the best in me."

CONTEMPLATION

Even the smallest tasks become special when we understand why we are doing them. With understanding comes respect. To respect something is to place a value on it: when we value what we do, we automatically give our best to the task at hand.

APPLICATION

Sometimes I have so many things to do that I tend to rush through them as quickly as possible, particularly those I don't rate as so important. I need to tell myself at the beginning of the day that today I will take the time to do everything properly, and enjoy what I do. This practice will help bring out the best in me.

DAY 292

VALUE: INTROSPECTION

"Introspection helps me to manage my thoughts better."

CONTEMPLATION

When we develop the practice of introspection, we find it easier to manage our thoughts as the mind becomes free of negativity. We find we spend less time thinking, since the right thoughts and solutions to problems emerge effortlessly.

APPLICATION

When I find myself thinking too much and going over a particular situation in my mind, I should try and sit in silence and practise going within myself instead. When I learn to experience the peace deep within me I will be able to remain calm and positive at all times.

Day 293

Value: Patience

"Patience helps me move beyond expectations."

Contemplation

Patience teaches us to sow the seed in the form of the right actions and to allow the fruits of those actions to ripen in their own time.

Application

I don't need to think about the future benefits of what I do now, because I know I will receive what I need when the time is right. If I let go of expectations and allow things to develop in their own time, I will be able to enjoy the tasks I do now for their own sake. The more enjoyment I get out of every activity, the better I will do.

DAY 294

VALUE: PEACE

"To experience peace is to become powerful."

CONTEMPLATION

Often, when we are busy and have a lot to remember, the mind becomes full of thoughts. The more the thoughts we have, the less peaceful the mind becomes. We can calm the mind by channeling our thoughts. By maintaining one powerful thought throughout the day, we can experience constant peace.

APPLICATION

In the morning, when my mind is calm, I need to focus on a positive, powerful thought, for example, "I am always fortunate". If I keep reminding myself of this thought, it will help me remain peaceful within myself, no matter what happens during the day.

DAY 295

VALUE: RESPONSIBILITY

"Responsibility is best fulfilled by the one who is detached."

CONTEMPLATION

It is easy we get too involved in a task we are responsible for, insisting on trying to do everything on our own. This only leads to us becoming more and more stressed and worried about the task, and stops us doing as well as we are able.

APPLICATION

When I have to take up some new responsibility, I need to tell myself that I will do my best in fulfilling the responsibility and then become detached. I will then find it easier to delegate and I will find myself doing my best because there are no expectations.

DAY 296

VALUE: DETERMINATION

"A victorious soul embodies success."

CONTEMPLATION

As soon as we have a thought, it is easy to let it fly away. We think we will attend to it in the future and tend to put off action. This is a sign of weakness.

APPLICATION

Today I will show determination with every thought that comes to mind. As soon as I have a thought I will become the embodiment of that thought. In this way I will also embody success.

DAY 297

VALUE: COMPASSION

"The one who is compassionate is constantly giving."

CONTEMPLATION

Compassion helps us understand other people around us. It allows us to forgive them for their mistakes, and to focus on what we can give them, rather than looking for something from them. Then we do not judge or try to change their behavior directly. Instead, we focus on their positive qualities and offer them our unconditional love.

APPLICATION

It is easy to judge people quickly without understanding the reasons behind their words or actions. When I am expecting others to change, I must remind myself that I am the one who must change because I understand the situation better. I can forgive others with love and only have good wishes for them. In turn, this will help them grow.

DAY 298

VALUE: RESPECT

"Respect is to recognize and appreciate the unique role of everyone."

CONTEMPLATION

Like actors, each of us plays a number of roles. In fact, we often play several roles at once, as we interact with different people in different settings. We need to realize that everyone is unique: no-one person could play another's part. Our respect for everyone grows when we understand this and recognize the individual contribution they make.

APPLICATION

When I find myself having negative thoughts toward anyone, I need to look at the special role this person has to play. When I look closely, I will realize how talented they are, and will develop new respect for them. Without this particular person, the drama of life would not be complete.

DAY 299

VALUE: TIRELESSNESS

"The one who is tireless works quietly to make changes in
themselves and others."

CONTEMPLATION

When things go wrong, tirelessness enables me to work toward
bringing about a change without complaining. Like when we
add bricks to build a foundation, no one notices the actual
work, but the result speaks for itself.

APPLICATION

Sometimes it can be difficult to adjust, especially when the
adjustment required is due to someone else's mistake. When
this happens, I have to have faith that this is my contribution to
bring about a change. When I adjust and adapt to the situation
without feelings of negativity, I will find things changing for
the better.

DAY 300

VALUE: COMPASSION

"Compassion is to give blessings to others."

CONTEMPLATION

When I have mercy for others I will not speak or think of the mistakes or the weaknesses in others. When I speak about such things, it spreads from one person to the next. Instead of speaking, I have to merge it into love. This sends blessing to others, which helps them improve.

APPLICATION

When I notice a weakness in someone, instead of drawing attention to it by speaking to others, I need to make a special effort to focus on something positive in that person. When I think about this person's good qualities, my love for them will grow. I will be able to see them in a positive light, whatever their flaws.

Day 301

Value: Responsibility

"Being responsible means performing one's role to the best of one's ability."

Contemplation

Just as an actor accepts the role he is given and performs to the best of his or her ability, so taking responsibility for one's life means accepting and honoring the role so that the performance is of the best quality. When we do this, we remain constantly aware of our time and resources, and use them as best we can.

Application

Each day I need to think of myself as a good actor who brings out the best in whatever role they are given. Instead of thinking about what I don't have, I need to accept responsibility for my life and honor the role so that my performance is the best.

Day 302

Value: Constancy

"The one who destroys all attachment becomes completely steady and constant."

Contemplation

It's easy to become attached – to money, to jewellery or relationships. But whatever we are attached to will draw our intellect toward it. When the intellect is pulled again and again it becomes impossible to remain constant.

Application

Today I will not let my intellect be pulled away from the matter in hand or allow my thoughts to wander aimlessly. This will help me to become more steady and constant in everything I do.

DAY 303

VALUE: RESPONSIBILITY

"The one who is responsible is the one who is satisfied."

CONTEMPLATION

When we grasp our responsibilities with enthusiasm and fulfill them with commitment, our work will become more efficient and effective. This leads to satisfaction and contentment.

APPLICATION

I need to take the responsibility to contribute something significant to every task I do. When I focus on this, I will find that I am able to give my best, and in turn I will be satisfied with whatever I am doing.

DAY 304

VALUE: SIMPLICITY

"Simplicity sharpens the power of perception."

CONTEMPLATION

Often, something we perceive as a big problem is actually much smaller than we realize. It is only when we get to the heart of the matter that we begin to understand that everything else was unimportant.

APPLICATION

Before I take any important decision I need to stop for a while, detach myself from the situation and consider it with a calm mind. When I do this, I will be able to look at the problem simply. My thoughts will become free from distractions and I will be able to make the right decision.

Day 305

Value: Stability

"Stability comes where there is truth."

Contemplation

If we ever find ourselves arguing to prove ourselves right, we are not truly stable. Of course, it may be necessary to clarify something for accuracy, but it should never be necessary to argue with stubbornness. If we argue, it means we are not convinced about the truth.

Application

When involved in an argument with someone, I need to check if I am convinced of the truth of what I am arguing about. If I am sure, then I need to remind myself that I needn't argue because truth will be revealed on its own at the right time. This will ensure my stability in that particular situation and I'll find things slowly becoming right.

Day 306

Value: Compassion

"True compassion is inclusive."

Contemplation

Real compassion is not just for one person, or a group of people, but for everyone. To learn what compassion means, we first need to understand that all human beings are in need, and we all have our own particular weaknesses. True compassion means freeing ourselves from our prejudices to reach out to those in need.

Application

While I am keen to help others, I am often discriminatory in who I choose to help. I need to try and reach out to whoever is in need, regardless of my own feelings toward them. When I am able to help others without judging them, I will be truly compassionate.

DAY 307

VALUE: SWEETNESS

"Sweetness is the ability to see the good in all things."

CONTEMPLATION

Deep within each and every situation is something good. It only takes a little patience to look within and find it. When we are able to understand the secret behind what is happening, it brings sweetness into our lives and enables us to move forward with lightness.

APPLICATION

Although some situations may seem negative, if I look harder, I will usually be able to find the sweetness hidden within. If I cannot see anything good in a particular situation, I need to have faith that it will be revealed at the right time, and that whatever happens is for the best. This practice helps me to enjoy the sweetness of life.

DAY 308

VALUE: PURITY

"Purity brings concentration."

CONTEMPLATION

When we are pure, we are free from careless thoughts. We become able to focus our thoughts on whatever we want to, whenever we want to. We become free from the wandering of the mind and will find it easy to concentrate, which allows us to achieve anything we set out to do more easily.

APPLICATION

When I am unable to concentrate on a task or when I find my mind wandering, I need to ask myself whether I am pure and positive within myself. I need to work on and remove even the slightest bit of negativity. Then I will be able to concentrate easily on whatever I set my mind to.

Day 309

Value: Humility

"To accept criticism positively is to learn and progress in life."

Contemplation

When others criticize us, we tend to react negatively toward them, even if we know they are only trying to help. By refusing to accept that they are trying to help us, we close ourselves off to learning. This means we are likely to keep making the same mistakes, and may even give up trying to progress.

Application

However hard I try, I cannot see myself as objectively as others can. If someone offers me constructive criticism, I should try and accept what they have to say with good grace, and be grateful that they care enough to try to help me. Only when I develop the humility to learn will I be able to progress.

DAY 310

VALUE: INTROSPECTION

"Introspection helps me get in touch with my pure, original and perfect self."

CONTEMPLATION

Introspection means spending time in silence and enables us to get in touch with our own pure, original and perfect self. It helps us to go within and recognize our own inner truth. The more we understand ourselves, the more able we are to deal with the world and the situations that arise in a positive way.

APPLICATION

I need to take the time to look within myself and see my own inner worth. Developing this practice will help me through even the most difficult times. It will help me maintain my self-respect and remain stable and happy whatever situation I find myself in.

DAY 311

VALUE: STABILITY

"Detachment brings stability."

CONTEMPLATION

When I use resources at home and work with detachment, I will
not be influenced by them but will make full use of them. When
I am attached to these instruments – perhaps a car, phone or
computer – I will not be able to remain stable when those
resources are not available for me to use. This is dependency.

APPLICATION

If ever find myself in a situation where some resource I use is not
available, I need to remind myself that items such as cars, phones
and computers do not create my responses to people and situations. These come from within me; the machines just facilitate my
response, and so I need not be dependent on them. In this way I
can be detached and maintain stability in all situations.

DAY 312

VALUE: TIRELESSNESS

"Tirelessness comes to those who are aware of the importance
of time."

CONTEMPLATION

Time passes quickly. Sometimes it is easy to forget how
important it is to make the most of each and every moment, and
we allow ourselves to become tired or bored. But when we
understand the importance of time, we become aware of the
importance of life.

APPLICATION

If I find myself caught up thinking about the past, I must
remind myself of the importance of the present moment. Only
the present is in my hands. When I learn to treasure the present
moment, and aim to use it in the right way, I will become
naturally tireless in my efforts.

DAY 313

VALUE: TOLERANCE

"When there is love, tolerance becomes easy."

CONTEMPLATION

Love frees us from expectations, enabling us to accept people as they are. When we look deep within and learn to love ourselves we grow strong. Understanding ourselves leads to understanding others, and then tolerance follows naturally.

APPLICATION

I need to think of one person in whom I see some quality that I struggle to tolerate. Then I need to remind myself that, just as a mother accepts her child despite its weaknesses and infirmities, I will accept this person as he or she is. When I learn to love that person for who they are, I will become tolerant.

DAY 314

VALUE: TRUST

"Trust grows from truth."

CONTEMPLATION

It can be difficult to learn who to trust. When we have had bad experiences with people who betrayed our trust in the past, it can be difficult to let anyone else in. It can take some time to learn to trust anyone again.

APPLICATION

Trust goes both ways. If I want to gain someone's trust, I have to show them that I trust them before he or she will open up to me. When I am truthful, this will be evident in everything I say and do. When others realize this, they will begin to trust me. From trust, love begins to grow.

Day 315

Value: Respect

"Respect for others enables them to strengthen themselves
and progress."

Contemplation

When we have respect for others, we create a positive
environment in which they can strengthen themselves and
grow. By focusing on their positive qualities, we encourage
them to take control of their own success.

Application

When I see someone trying hard to improve themselves, I need
to show my respect for them by thinking of ways in which I can
support them. Everyone needs help to fulfill their potential. I
can offer support in a variety of ways, from simply listening to
another person's ideas to offering them constructive criticism or
practical help. Then we will all benefit from their good wishes,
and the skills they share.

DAY 316

VALUE: SIMPLICITY

"The one who lives a simple life is free from pain."

CONTEMPLATION

Learning to live in a simple way means learning to see things clearly. We have a choice about how we see things – the best choice is to concentrate on what is important and detach ourselves from what is not. Then we can let go of the negative feelings associated with the past, and remember only what we have learned from it.

APPLICATION

Living a simple life means focusing on the things that can help me, and letting go of those that bring suffering. When something goes wrong today I need to focus on thoughts and actions that help me see clearly in the present.

DAY 317

VALUE: HOPE

"To transform negativity into hope brings progress."

CONTEMPLATION

When someone behaves negatively toward us, we get disturbed and upset. Although we try to stay calm and balanced, our own negative feelings make the situation worse. When this happens, we find ourselves losing hope, and then there is no benefit in anything we think, speak or do.

APPLICATION

The only way I can remain positive and experience progress in the most negative situation is to hold on to hope. I need to understand that no situation is ever totally negative or completely without hope. This will give me the strength to look at the situation more closely and find the positive hidden within it.

DAY 318

VALUE: LIGHTNESS

"To experience lightness is to let go of our burdens."

CONTEMPLATION

When we have a problem, we usually carry the entire weight of it ourselves. We sometimes feel that to ask for help is to admit weakness. We find it difficult to let go, even though the weight of the problem is bringing us down and making it difficult for us to enjoy life.

APPLICATION

I need to look at the burden I am carrying around with me and work out if there is a way to lighten the load, or even to get rid of it all together. Sometimes, sharing a problem with others is the easiest way to take the weight off my shoulders. Then I will begin to experience lightness and this will enable me to find the right solutions.

DAY 319

VALUE: TOLERANCE

"The one who is tolerant is most successful."

CONTEMPLATION

Tolerance frees the mind of careless thoughts because then we experience no negativity toward anyone. When we are tolerant, we are accepting of others and situations. This means we adapt easily and will soon achieve success.

APPLICATION

When things go wrong and I find obstacles in my way, instead of worrying or sinking into negativity, I need draw upon the power of tolerance to help me accept the situation. When I have acknowledged that I cannot change what has happened, I am freed to focus on the solution.

DAY 320

VALUE: FREEDOM

"The desire for perfection ends all other desires."

CONTEMPLATION

Our life is full of desires. When one desire is fulfilled, ten others take its place in a never-ending cycle. We tend to get disturbed or upset when our desires are not fulfilled, yet we often continue to justify them. Life then becomes full of expectation followed by disappointment. We become slaves to our desires.

APPLICATION

The desire for perfection only brings the capacity to keep learning from all situations. Since the mind is busy bringing about perfection, there is no time for negativity. I no longer think about what I want to obtain, but continue to gain through the knowledge I accumulate. Then I become free from all other desires, and experience progress.

Day 321

Value: Appreciation

"To be careless means to misuse our gifts."

Contemplation

We are often careless with our gifts. Sometimes we misuse them or neglect them. We often rely on certain gifts to get us through, rather than making effort to address situations properly. We become careless, and unable to recognize the need for self-development.

Application

I need to understand the importance of the gifts I have been given, and that they have been given to me for a reason. I will remind myself today not to take them for granted. Instead, I will use my abilities to try to help others as well as myself. The more my gifts develop, the more quickly I will grow.

Day 322

Value: Courage

"The one who has the power to face situations with courage is free from tension."

Contemplation

It is natural to feel worry or tension in a difficult situation – or to run away from the situation altogether. Although this may work for a short time, it is not a solution. We have to draw upon our inner courage in order to meet the challenge head on. When we do this, we often realize it is not as bad as it first appeared.

Application

Courage drives out fear and negativity. When I can face every situation with courage, I will no longer encounter difficulties. I will become free from tension, and better able to tackle anything that life throws at me.

DAY 323

VALUE: DISCERNMENT

"Feelings change intentions, which in turn change actions."

CONTEMPLATION

Everything we do is affected by how we feel about it, even if we are unaware of our feelings at the time. Sometimes we are caught up with negative feelings, such as jealousy or hatred of another person. These feelings create misunderstanding and conflict. Even if the other person does something with good intentions, we may not be able to see this.

APPLICATION

Instead of being caught up with negative feelings, I need to look for the positive in everything and make the effort to understand my feelings. When I start seeing the world in a different way, this will affect the things I do. I will start behaving positively toward others, and this will affect their behavior toward me.

DAY 324

VALUE: AWARENESS

"An elevated consciousness brings specialty to the task being done."

CONTEMPLATION

Sometimes, while engaged in a special task, our consciousness tends to become ordinary because of negative feelings for the self or others. Such thoughts turn even the most special task into an ordinary one.

APPLICATION

I need to understand that my consciousness (or how I feel about something) affects what I do. If I feel negatively toward it, the quality of what I produce will drop. When I am able to start each task with a special consciousness, thinking "I am creative", or "I am happy" or even "this task is for the benefit of all", I become fully aware and able to appreciate the experience of doing the task. This allows me to carry out the task to the best of my ability.

DAY 325

VALUE: SELF-CONTROL

"To be free from careless words ensures easy success."

CONTEMPLATION

We often waste a lot of time and energy in gossip or slander. We focus on pointing out the mistakes of others rather than paying attention to learning new things or looking for the positive. When our attitude, words and actions are full of negativity, there can be no real success.

APPLICATION

When I free myself from careless words and a negative attitude, I will be able to use my resources in a positive and useful way. If I believe in myself and others, the words I speak will be filled with the power of faith and positivity. I will soon find I accomplish much more, and receive the good wishes of those around me.

DAY 326

VALUE: POSITIVITY

"To be free from questions brings the ability to fly."

CONTEMPLATION

When difficult situations come our way, we tend to create a lot of unnecessary questions in our minds. These wasteful thoughts fill our minds with negativity, draining us of energy. At the time, it seems natural to have such thoughts and we get caught up only with these ideas, leaving no space for constructive thoughts.

APPLICATION

When difficult situations come my way, I need not be caught up with "why" things happened, but instead make the effort to "fly". I need to find a way to empower myself so that I become stronger than the situation; so that I can fly above it. Then the situation will seem tiny and I can overcome it easily.

Day 327

Value: Self-control

"To progress is to be careful with one's inner resources."

Contemplation

We usually pay attention to accumulating wealth and take care not to waste money. But we rarely think about how we waste time or thoughts.

Application

Every day I need to check where and how I use my two main resources: time and thoughts. When I am aware of how I spend them, I will realize where I use them well, and when I could make better use of them. Constant checking will help me use them in a more constructive way and I will soon notice how much more easily I progress in all my tasks.

DAY 328

VALUE: GIVING

"The way to get what we need is to give."

CONTEMPLATION

We usually want to get the best out of everything. We have expectations about what we feel we should receive. But sometimes we find it difficult to get what we need. We may try harder, but still find ourselves unable to get the best out of people or situations. This only leads to frustration.

APPLICATION

If I am not getting what I want or need, I may need to adopt a different approach. Instead of focusing on my own desires, I need to understand that perhaps I'm not getting what I want for a reason – perhaps I'm not ready for it yet. If I concentrate instead on what I have to give others, I will find that what I need comes to me naturally.

DAY 329

VALUE: SELF-CONTROL

"To be free from careless words is to be light."

CONTEMPLATION

While we tend to avoid saying things that are negative or harmful toward others, we often speak carelessly. Sometimes we say things that are of no use to others, or may even hurt their feelings. Careless words weigh us down and stop us from feeling light and free.

APPLICATION

I need to pay attention so that I so not speak carelessly. If I keep in mind the phrase "Speak less, speak softly and speak sweetly", this little thought will help me make my words more meaningful and I will never hurt others' feelings.

DAY 330

VALUE: CALMNESS

"To be calm is to work to build relationships."

CONTEMPLATION

It is easy to speak negatively when we do not like something about someone and to react to a situation and become angry. The other person naturally responds negatively to our negative thoughts, and then it becomes almost impossible to build a positive relationship.

APPLICATION

When something goes wrong in any relationship, the first thing I need to do is to keep calm. When I do this, I will not be caught up with the negativity of the situation or the negative trait of the person at that time. Instead I will be able to see the beauty in that person. I will be able to appreciate and connect to the uniqueness of that person and so create a positive atmosphere that helps to rebuild the relationship.

DAY 331

VALUE: BALANCE

"With the balance of love and discipline, energy can be saved while speaking."

CONTEMPLATION

Throughout the day, we find ourselves having to explain many things to many people. In doing so, we expend a lot of words. In the process, we tend to lose a great deal of energy and become tired. It is not the work but the words that make us feel tired.

APPLICATION

In order to save my energy and use fewer words I need to make sure I maintain the balance of love and discipline when explaining things to others. Discipline will equip me to give the right directions while love will make my directions effective. I will soon find that a few words are enough to get my message across.

DAY 332

VALUE: GIVING

"To be a giver is to be powerful."

CONTEMPLATION

It is easy to give to those who are positive toward us. It is more difficult to recognize that those who behave negatively toward us are often more in need of our help.

APPLICATION

The only way I can remain positive when someone is behaving negatively toward me is to remind myself of my inner power. When I connect to what I have, I am able to be a giver without expecting anything in return. The cool waters of my positivity help put out the fire of anger.

DAY 333

VALUE: SELF-CONTROL

"To be free from desires is to be full of all attainments."

CONTEMPLATION

Although we are generally free from big desires we are often full of little desires. Even though they are only small, they have a noticeable effect on our well-being: because of these little desires we are not able to experience and enjoy all life's attainments.

APPLICATION

I need to tell myself that chasing desires is like chasing my own shadow: the more I try to follow it, the more it runs away from me. All I have to do is to turn back and move toward the sun (my destination). Then my shadow will follow me and I will feel contented and fulfilled.

DAY 334

VALUE: LOVE

"Self-love brings joy to one's life."

CONTEMPLATION

People look for love through relationships. Yet this love is colored with expectation. When these expectations are not fulfilled there is a tendency to get upset. Before we can love others, we need to learn to love ourselves.

APPLICATION

When I love myself, I am able to appreciate all the unique qualities and virtues that are part of me. I feel happy and secure within myself, and I am able to project that love out toward other people. The more love I express, the more love I receive in return, filling my life with joy.

DAY 335

VALUE: GIVING

"To help others to grow is to enable ourselves to grow."

CONTEMPLATION

It is easy to raise our voices and complain when we encounter someone else's negativity. This disturbs our own inner calm, and we become caught up with that negativity. When thrown off-balance in this way, we are unable to give the other person the support he or she needs.

APPLICATION

When someone is doing something wrong, I need to see what I can do to help that person. There is surely something I can contribute toward the growth of each and every human being. When I focus on how best to offer my help, I do not become caught up with negativity, and I can transform the situation into one that benefits us both.

DAY 336

VALUE: POSITIVITY

"The vision of seeing specialties frees the mind from
negativity."

CONTEMPLATION

Negativity is more easily noticed than positivity. Whenever we
see someone using some negative trait, all their specialties
remain hidden and we get caught up with their negativity. Our
interactions with that person become tainted by negativity, and
it becomes difficult to turn things around.

APPLICATION

I need to focus on seeing the positive in the people around me.
When someone does or says something negative, I need to make
a special effort to see something good. This helps me to keep
myself free from negativity and makes my interaction with that
person pleasant, rather than fraught with difficulties. The other
person is likely to respond positively toward me, which in turn
will help them leave their negativity behind.

DAY 337

VALUE: COMMUNICATION

"The language of thoughts is more powerful than the language of words."

CONTEMPLATION

When we have a misunderstanding with someone, we often talk a lot to try and explain our point of view. But we have a tendency to become defensive when we feel threatened, and often words only make the situation worse. Rather than talking more, we need to learn to think better.

APPLICATION

I know that sometimes it is not my words that are important, but the thoughts behind them. I may say little, but the feeling behind my words is so strong that it is easy for the other person to understand my intentions. Powerful thoughts bring clarity to my communication with others, and help me develop my relationships.

DAY 338

VALUE: PURITY

"To invoke the goodness within is to be pure."

CONTEMPLATION

Deep within ourselves, we have a lot of goodness. When we are pure, we will find we are able to work with our inherent goodness. Then nothing negative can prevent us from expressing it. We become a clean mirror that allows others to see their own image of perfection.

APPLICATION

I need to remind myself that when I work on my inner purity I can help people get in touch with their inherent goodness, too. When I encounter someone negative, it is my duty to work with them to help them experience their original goodness. When I remind myself of this, I make myself a clean mirror.

DAY 339

VALUE: PATIENCE

"The one who is patient experiences constant success."

CONTEMPLATION

We often expect things to happen quickly. Even if we only put in a little effort we expect big results. If we lack patience, we often jump to conclusions and react without understanding the situation. When this happens, we are much less likely to succeed.

APPLICATION

I need to understand that the fruit of the seeds I sow will come in time. This gives me the patience to wait without expecting results too fast. Patience also helps me to remain calm in the most negative situations. When I become patient I will experience success whatever the immediate result of my actions might be.

DAY 340

VALUE: POSITIVITY

"To see the unique qualities in everyone is to become special."

CONTEMPLATION

Although someone may have many positive qualities, as soon as we notice one negative quality in them we find it difficult to see anything else. What we see in someone affects how we feel about them, and our relationships can suffer because of this.

APPLICATION

It is natural to be colored or influenced by what I see. But I have the power within me to change my perception. When I choose to focus on the positive, I gradually forget about other people's flaws. As I learn to appreciate them for their gifts and virtues, our relationship also becomes stronger.

DAY 341

VALUE: CREATIVITY

"To be creative is to bring newness at each step."

CONTEMPLATION

Sometimes we have a tendency to get bored with what we are doing. Even when working toward a goal, and moving continuously toward it, we are not satisfied. The days seem to drag without bringing any real joy. When this happens, we may question what we are doing, or even be tempted to give up.

APPLICATION

I need to be creative and try to bring something new to what I am doing every day. Even a small change can make a big difference. When I think creatively, I become more enthusiastic about what I am doing, and then there will always be something interesting to look forward to.

DAY 342

VALUE: LOVE

"Love allows us to experience victory in all situations".

CONTEMPLATION

Love gives us strength to draw upon in times of need and equips us to move forward with courage to tackle all the challenges life brings. When we love others and are loved in return, we will always be victorious.

APPLICATION

In a situation in which I find myself failing, I should draw strength from the love that surrounds me, as well as the love within me. Knowing I am loved gives me the faith to overcome whatever obstacles are in my way. When others love me, my belief in myself increases, leading to success.

Day 343

Value: Introspection

"My power enables me to look after and use the treasures within me."

Contemplation

Within every one of us there are a many treasures – thoughts, powers, values and virtues. We may be unaware of some of them, or not be using them to their full potential. But when we look within ourselves, we gradually become aware of these treasures, and learn how to use them in a worthwhile way.

Application

I need to explore the treasures within me and try to discover one that I can work on today. The more I work with the gifts I have been given, the stronger they will become.

Day 344

Value: Contribution

"To contribute selflessly is to move forward with the blessings of all."

Contemplation

Sometimes we find ourselves in situations in which there is a problem – where we are part of that problem. When we try defending ourselves, others do not always understand. At such times it seems as if there is no solution, and we find ourselves going in circles.

Application

I need to become part of the solution instead of the problem, even if it does not benefit me personally. This means doing whatever I can – no matter how small – in order to better the situation. When I contribute to the solution, I create positive energy for change and receive blessings from those around me.

DAY 345

VALUE: PURITY

"The one who is pure wins the hearts of others."

CONTEMPLATION

To be pure means to be without negative feelings or attitudes. When we are pure, we are full of good wishes for others. This naturally attracts others' love and blessings.

APPLICATION

I need to try to remain pure in all my thoughts, words and actions today. This practice helps to keep me free from negativity. I must try to have good wishes for everyone I encounter, regardless of how they behave toward me. When I am pure, I naturally attract good things into my life.

Day 346

Value: Sweetness

"Others experience sweetness when words are filled with the power of truth."

Contemplation

The world is filled with false sweetness – for example, we may praise someone for having done well without really understanding what they've achieved. This does not really benefit anyone. For our words to have a real and lasting effect, sweetness must be combined with truth.

Application

In order for my words to have an effect on others, I must take time to see if I have really understood the goodness in the other person. Everything I say should be based only on the truth I have discovered in others. Words that are spoken from the heart are always effective, and spread sweetness throughout my life and the lives of those around me.

DAY 347

VALUE: FORGIVENESS

"To forgive is to use the power of love within me."

CONTEMPLATION

When we have a difference of opinion with someone, we may not be able to express any love for that person. If we find it difficult to talk to or interact with that person, we may try to get round the situation by avoiding them altogether. The longer this goes on, the more difficult it becomes for us to forgive them.

APPLICATION

My feelings for others reveal that I have the power of love within me. I just need to learn to bring out this love. Love will help me remember all the positive qualities others have, and I will soon find I am able to forgive them and make amends.

DAY 348

VALUE: APPRECIATION

"The one who is free from the desire for fame and glory receives natural recognition."

CONTEMPLATION

When we make a positive contribution, we often expect to get some sort of recognition. Although we rarely voice this opinion, we feel hurt if others fail to show their appreciation for what we have done.

APPLICATION

It's easy to get caught up in doing things just to get praise or recognition. This means I don't really focus on what I'm actually doing, or doing it for the right reasons. If I make sure that I enjoy whatever I do, I will no longer be concerned with gaining recognition, but will be able to enjoy the task for its own sake.

DAY 349

VALUE: ENTHUSIASM

"To remain constantly enthusiastic means exchanging ideas
with others."

CONTEMPLATION

Often when we are working toward a task, we find ourselves
losing enthusiasm. Things become dull or routine and our work
suffers. Other people become unhappy with us or our work.
While we try to understand their feelings, this is difficult, and
our enthusiasm drops even further.

APPLICATION

When I find myself losing enthusiasm, I need to ask myself if I
can approach the task in another way. Just talking about what I
am doing with someone else can help me feel positive about it
again, and he or she may inspire me to try something new.
Through the exchange of ideas, I become excited about the task
once more, and my work quickly improves.

Day 350

Value: Self-control

"Where there is self-control there is flexibility."

Contemplation

When someone challenges the truth of what we say, we generally argue and try and prove ourselves right. If we are stubborn and unwilling to listen to anyone else's point of view, we miss out on the opportunity to learn, and may damage our relationships.

Application

Sometimes I am so convinced that I am right that I find it difficult to listen to someone else's point of view. I have to realize that even if I am right, there may be something I can learn from listening to another's point of view. I must take care to speak and listen respectfully in order to develop my relationships with others.

DAY 351

VALUE: PATIENCE

"Patience brings harmonious relationships."

CONTEMPLATION

Misunderstandings can cause problems in a relationship, especially when we make little effort to understand another person and their point of view. We tend to become impatient and do not listen to what the other person is saying. Instead, we make assumptions, which are often wrong and cause further misunderstandings.

APPLICATION

When I have a difference of opinion with someone, I need to make time to listen to what the other person has to say. Only then will I be able to understand their point of view. This practice will help me clear up any misunderstandings I have with others and bring harmony to my relationships.

DAY 352

VALUE: PROGRESS

"Real progress can be experienced when we face obstacles."

CONTEMPLATION

When we encounter obstacles along our path, we usually perceive them as negative and become irritated or discouraged. Our work suffers as a result. But it may be our attitude toward the obstacles that is the real problem, rather than the obstacles themselves.

APPLICATION

When I come across a difficultly, I often see it as something negative. Instead of seeing it as threat, I need to regard each new obstacle as an opportunity to stretch myself and develop my skills. If I only attempt things I know I can do easily, I will not experience progress. I need to keep in mind that to develop, I need to experience challenges on a regular basis.

DAY 353

VALUE: HONESTY

"To be honest with oneself is the only way to progress."

CONTEMPLATION

When we do not perform well, it is tempting to make excuses. One of the hardest things to learn is how to acknowledge our weaknesses. Until we are able to do this, we will continue deluding ourselves that we are something we are not, and we will never reach our full potential.

APPLICATION

When I am totally honest with myself, I will be able to see my weaknesses as clearly as in the mirror. Once I have accepted that I need to make changes, I will become motivated to succeed. Each small success will inspire me to the next step and I will continue to progress.

DAY 354

VALUE: CREATIVITY

"Inner satisfaction brings creativity."

CONTEMPLATION

We often find ourselves falling into a routine. We perform tasks the way we have always done them – often for no particular reason. Life becomes monotonous, and we find it difficult to become inspired.

APPLICATION

Only when I am happy within myself can I bring creativity to my life. Even though I have to do a number of routine jobs each day, they do not have to become dull – when I am happy, I can think of innovative ways of doing them. Even small changes have a big impact, and I will soon be inspired to make even larger changes to challenge me further.

Day 355

Value: Blessings

"The way to get blessings is to be open to learning."

Contemplation

When faced with negative situations, we often seek help or blessings from others. But when we ask for help it may not be forthcoming, and we wonder if we have done something wrong. Sometimes the help we really need is for others to leave us to get on with things – we have to learn from our own mistakes.

Application

I need to learn that the best way to bring blessings into my life is to take positive action. Even failure can be a blessing if it enables me to learn something. When I learn how to help myself, I will find that other people and situations conspire to help me.

DAY 356

VALUE: SELF-CONTROL

"To understand the importance of my actions is to create my own destiny."

CONTEMPLATION

We often blame the situation or other people when things go wrong. But sometimes we need to look inward and check whether there was anything we could have done differently. It can be difficult to acknowledge when we have made a mistake, but this is the only way we can learn to be truly successful.

APPLICATION

Instead of blaming the situation or other people when things go wrong, I need to understand that power lies in my own hands. When I am honest with myself, I can learn from past situations. I have the power to put things right, and the ability to achieve whatever I put my mind to.

DAY 357

VALUE: INNER POWER

"To be an embodiment of power is to be free from effort."

CONTEMPLATION

When faced with a challenge, we try to fill our mind with positive thoughts in an effort to combat the negativity of the situation. If we find this difficult, we start to believe that we don't have the power to change our nature. Then we continue to work with the weakness and strengthen it further.

APPLICATION

In order to overcome my weaknesses I need to become an embodiment of power. To do this, I need to get used to working with my power and believing in myself. Then I will be able call on my inner power whenever I need it and transform a negative situation into a positive one with ease.

DAY 358

VALUE: INTROSPECTION

"The one who knows to look within finds solutions to all problems."

CONTEMPLATION

Whenever we are faced with a problem, we hope that something will happen to change the circumstances. When nothing happens, we begin to look for support or guidance from others. We rarely think to look within. Often the solutions we need are there; we just don't know how to find them.

APPLICATION

If something goes wrong, the first thing I need to do is calm my mind and look within. I need to have faith that the solutions to all problems lie within me. As long as I remain positive, I will find the answers I need.

Day 359

Value: Faith

"The one who overcomes situations using their inner power is a winner."

Contemplation

Sometimes situations come our way that we feel are too difficult for us even to attempt to solve. We need to remember that everything happens for a reason. Keeping this in mind makes the situation seem clearer, and brings solutions to the surface.

Application

Whenever I am faced with a situation that I feel is too big for me to tackle, I need to take a step back and look at it from a different angle. I need to have faith in my inner strength and remember that every situation has something to teach me, if I am willing to learn from it. Only when I have the faith and push myself to achieve will I be able to grow.

DAY 360

VALUE: DISCERNMENT

"True power lies in understanding the significance of every situation."

CONTEMPLATION

When a difficult situation comes up, lots of questions come to mind. We often find it hard to understand why a particular incident has happened, and this makes us feel helpless and confused. We can then do nothing to change the situation.

APPLICATION

I need to try to understand the significance of any situation that comes up. There is a reason behind every situation. When I can work out why the situation has happened, I will be able to work out what to do to resolve it. This will help me regain control, and give me the power to take care of it successfully.

DAY 361

VALUE: BLESSINGS

"The one who accumulates blessings at each step attains easy success."

CONTEMPLATION

While working toward a goal, we sometimes find ourselves becoming so focused on it that we forget about those around us. While we achieve what we set out to do, it is often at the cost of others' feelings and to the detriment of our relationships.

APPLICATION

Behind every success there is the support of a strong pillar of blessings. So I need to check how many people I make smile every day and think about what I could do to make those I care about happy. This will help me become more sensitive to the feelings of others and help me continue to receive their blessings and good wishes.

Day 362

VALUE: SUCCESS

"Where everything is done according to the right method there is success."

CONTEMPLATION

When we don't achieve success immediately, we sometimes get tempted to opt for a short cut. Although we might achieve something temporarily, in the long run it won't be beneficial – and sometimes has the opposite effect to the one we desire.

APPLICATION

Whenever I am involved in a task, I need to make sure that I am doing it properly. Although at times I might be tempted to cut corners, I know this will only cause me problems later on. When I make the effort to follow the right method, I know that it will be worthwhile in the end, and I will feel a greater sense of achievement when I complete the task.

DAY 363

VALUE: SELF-DISCIPLINE

"True discipline is easy and natural."

CONTEMPLATION

When we talk of discipline we usually think about something enforced on us. Self-discipline is something many of us struggle with; it is something we have to work hard at developing and maintaining. During times of need, we learn to discipline ourselves. But when the time passes, or the pressure is off, we tend to return to our normal pattern of behavior. Because it takes effort, self- discipline is considered difficult and burdensome.

APPLICATION

Self-discipline is an expression of respect for myself. The more I think about disciplining myself today, the stronger I will become.

Day 364

Value: Positivity

"To practise the power of positivity is to be free from
negativity."

Contemplation

Whenever we need to think positive in a situation, we try to
force the mind to think in that way. We force the mind into
thinking what we desire. Yet the mind is not capable of doing
that to order. So there are no positive results and we find
ourselves with more negativity.

Application

I need to be a mother to my mind, teaching it to think the right
kind of thoughts. Even when everything is going well, I need to
train the mind. Taking one positive thought every day and
spending time with it brings good results. This training makes
the mind obedient at the time of need and allows me to be
positive even in the most negative situations.

DAY 365

VALUE: SUCCESS

"Real success means experiencing internal progress."

CONTEMPLATION

The usual definition of success is connected with visible
success, such as profit, or increase in status. Success is also
understood as an ideal state in which nothing goes wrong. But
often we work hard without having much to show for our
efforts.

APPLICATION

It is more important to experience success within ourselves that
it is to accumulate wealth or other outward trappings of
success. When I put in the effort to improve myself and strive
to overcome my weaknesses, I will triumph. It will not matter
whether I appear successful on the outside or what others think
of me because I will know I have made real progress.

ABOUT RAJA YOGA

The Brahma Kumaris World Spiritual University is an international organization working at all levels of society for positive change. Established in 1937, the University now has more than 8,500 centres in over 100 countries.

Acknowledging the intrinsic worth and goodness of the inner self, the University teaches a practical method of meditation that helps people to cultivate their inner strengths and values.

The University has local centres around the world offering courses and seminars that encourage spirituality in daily life and cover topics such as positive thinking, anger management, stress relief and self-esteem, amongst others. This spiritual approach is also brought into healthcare, social work, education, prisons and other community settings.

The University's Academy in Mount Abu, Rajasthan, India, offers individuals from all backgrounds a variety of life-long learning opportunities to help them recognize their inherent qualities and abilities in order to make the most of their lives. The University also supports the Global Hospital and Research Centre in Mount Abu.

All courses and activities are offered free of charge.
www.bkwsu.org
www.bkwsu.org/uk

HOW TO FIND OUT MORE

WORLD HEADQUARTERS

PO Box No 2, Mount Abu 307501, RAJASTHAN, INDIA
Tel: (+91) 2974 - 238261 to 68 Fax: (+91) 2974 - 238883
E-mail: abu@bkivv.org

INTERNATIONAL CO-ORDINATING OFFICE & REGIONAL OFFICE FOR EUROPE AND THE MIDDLE EAST

Global Co-operation House, 65-69 Pound Lane, London, NW10
2HH, UK
Tel: (+44) 208 727 3350 Fax: (+44) 208 727 3351
E-mail: london@bkwsu.org

AFRICA

Global Museum for a Better World, Maua Close, off Parklands
Road, Westlands
PO Box 123, Sarit Centre, Nairobi, Kenya
Tel: (+254) 20-374 3572 Fax: (+254) 20-374 3885
E-mail: nairobi@bkwsu.org

AUSTRALIA AND SOUTH EAST ASIA

78 Alt Street, Ashfield, Sydney, NSW 2131, Australia
Tel: (+61) 2 9716 7066 Fax: (+61) 2 9716 7795
E-mail: ashfield@au.bkwsu.org

THE AMERICAS AND THE CARIBBEAN

Global Harmony House, 46 S. Middle Neck Road, Great Neck,
NY 11021, USA
Tel: (+1) 516 773 0971 Fax: (+1) 516 773 0976
E-mail: newyork@bkwsu.org

RUSSIA, CIS AND THE BALTIC COUNTRIES
2 Gospitalnaya Ploschad, build. 1, Moscow - 111020, Russia
Tel: (+7) 495 263 02 47 Fax: (+7) 495 261 32 24
E-mail: moscow@bkwsu.org

www.bkpublications.com
E-mail: enquiries@bkpublications.com

ABOUT THE AUTHOR

Dadi Janki provides inspiration to everyone she meets - she sees the highest potential in all human beings. She lovingly engages people of all faiths and walks of life to be true to their spiritual self, to undertake their unique and individual part in creating a future world worthy of the generations to come. Her wisdom and clarity come from a deep connection with God and her unfailing belief that there is good in everyone.

A visionary whose uniqueness lies in her unswerving optimism and a heart rich in compassion, Dadi Janki has redefined the concept of freedom in the West by placing it within the context of the ancient wisdom of the East. Internationally acknowledged as a great teacher and mentor, she continues to offer inspiration to many people who are searching for peace and harmony in their heart and in their homeland.

Dadi Janki maintains an unrivalled daily lecture and touring schedule even today, aged 95. She has travelled worldwide almost incessantly over the past 40 years, engaging with people at all levels, from grass roots to government leaders and royalty. She is someone who refuses to set limits and boundaries on what is achievable. In so doing, she inspires others to believe that they, too, can make the impossible possible. Since coming to the UK in the mid 1970s, she has been instrumental in overseeing the expansion of the work of the University worldwide - now in more than 120 countries.

Containing wisdom for every day of the year, this little book is something to keep with you at all times. Dadi Janki's understanding, depth of wisdom and insights are captured here to sustain and inspire everyone everyday.

BOOKS

O is a symbol of the world, of oneness and unity. In different cultures it also means the "eye," symbolizing knowledge and insight. We aim to publish books that are accessible, constructive and that challenge accepted opinion, both that of academia and the "moral majority."

Our books are available in all good English language bookstores worldwide. If you don't see the book on the shelves ask the bookstore to order it for you, quoting the ISBN number and title. Alternatively you can order online (all major online retail sites carry our titles) or contact the distributor in the relevant country, listed on the copyright page.

See our website **www.o-books.net** for a full list of over 500 titles, growing by 100 a year.

And tune in to myspiritradio.com for our book review radio show, hosted by June-Elleni Laine, where you can listen to the authors discussing their books.

mySpiritRadio